Editors
Sara Connolly
Maria Gallardo, M.A.

Illustrator
Clint McKnight

Cover Artist
Brenda DiAntonis

Editor in Chief
Ina Massler Levin, M.A.

Creative Director
Karen J. Goldfluss, M.S. Ed.

Art Production Manager
Kevin Barnes

Art Coordinator
Renée Christine Yates

Imaging
Craig Gunnell
Nathan P. Riivera
James Edward Grace

Publisher
Mary D. Smith, M.S. Ed.

Prepa

STANDARDIZED TESTS

Grade 4

LANGUAGE ARTS

MATH

SOCIAL STUDIES

SCIENCE

Includes Standards

Includes a variety of strategies for successful test taking

Offers helpful tips and suggestions to reduce test anxiety

Author

Julia McMeans, M. Ed.

Teacher Created Resources, Inc.
6421 Industry Way
Westminster, CA 92683
www.teachercreated.com
ISBN: 978-1-4206-2894-4
©2009 Teacher Created Resources, Inc.
Reprinted, 2014
Made in U.S.A.

Teacher Created Resources

Table of Contents

Introduction

Standardized tests have not only been the subject of intense controversy among educators, but also the cause of much teeth gnashing among students. If individuals are unique, and learning styles and ways of understanding vary, how then can a standardized test accurately measure what a student knows?

There is a story of a first-grade teacher who held up a red apple to her class of 30 eager students and asked, "What color is this apple?" Twenty-nine of the students replied, "It's red," while one brave soul countered, "It's red and white." "Oh," the teacher responded, "I don't see any white," to which the student replied, "That's because you have to bite it!"

This is a cautionary tale that demonstrates that there are multiple ways in which to know, and that they can all potentially be correct. For this reason, it is critical that both educators and students understand what standardized tests seek to measure and the best strategies to prepare for and take these kinds of tests.

The vast majority of standardized tests that students encounter during their academic careers, including the California Achievement Test, the Iowa Test, and the Stanford Achievement Test, are norm-referenced tests. Norm-referenced tests compare and rank students in a particular grade with other students in that same grade. By doing this, educators can get a quick snapshot of where their students stand and to what extent their scores deviate from the average or the norm.

The content contained in standardized tests is aligned with state-wide curriculum standards, and vice versa. If a skill set appears in your content standards, it is reasonable to expect that it may appear on a standardized test. For example, you will never find a problem such as this on a fourth-grade standardized test:

$(4x - 2x^2 - 7xy) + (2x^2 + 5xy)$

However, you would very likely find a problem like this: 63 x 59.

The reason is clear—the addition and subtraction of polynomials is not part of the fourth-grade core content for math, while the multiplication of two-digit numbers is.

It is imperative that students understand how standardized tests are scored, what they measure, and the kind of material they will encounter. By sharing this behind-the-scenes aspect of standardized tests with your students, you will help to empower them by demystifying the tests themselves, and thus reducing the high anxiety often associated with them.

Standardized tests can be an effective measurement tool. Over the years, great steps have been taken not only to improve standardized testing—for instance, paying particular attention to bias in order to create tests that are more equitable—but also to provide students with an array of strategies that they can use in test-taking situations.

The purpose of this book is to help educators and students prepare for standardized tests by providing general information on test-taking strategies, tips on stress and anxiety reduction, and a variety of practice tests that span the core content that appears on these types of tests.

The practice tests contained within this book are arranged according to content area and then by specific skill sets within that area. The test questions are written in the style most frequently used on standardized tests and are aligned with the McRel Compendium of Content Standards. Blank student answer sheets can be found on page 135.

McRel Compendium of Content Standards and Skills Index

Content Area	Standards Covered	Specific Skills Covered
Writing	• Uses the general skills and strategies of the writing process. • Uses the stylistic and rhetorical aspects of writing. • Uses grammatical and mechanical conventions in written compositions. • Gathers and uses information for research purposes.	Capitalization • Combining • Conjugation • Contractions • Editing • Elaborating • Paragraphing • Pronoun Referents • Punctuation • Spelling • Subject-Verb Agreement • Types of Sentences • Usage
Reading	• Uses the general skills and strategies of the reading process. • Uses reading skills and strategies to understand and interpret a variety of literary texts. • Uses reading skills and strategies to understand and interpret a variety of informational texts.	**Reading Comprehension:** Author's Purpose • Cause and Effect • Compare and Contrast • Conflict • Fact versus Opinion • Fiction • Figurative Language • Inferences • Main Idea • Nonfiction • Plot • Poetry • Point of View • Prediction • Literary Genres • Research • Rhyming • Sequencing • Setting • Supporting Details • Topic Sentence **Vocabulary** Affixes • Antonyms • Homographs • Syllabication • Synonyms
Math	• Uses a variety of strategies in the problem solving process. • Understands and applies basic and advanced properties of the concepts of numbers. • Uses basic and advanced procedures while performing the processes of computation. • Understands and applies basic and advanced properties of the concepts of measurement. • Understands and applies basic and advanced properties of the concepts of geometry. • Understands and applies basic and advanced properties of the concepts of statistics and data analysis. • Understands and applies basic and advanced properties of the concepts of probability. • Understands and applies basic and advanced properties of functions and algebra. • Understands the general nature and uses of mathematics.	**Number Concepts:** Prime and Composite Numbers • Factors and Multiples • Odd and Even Numbers • Equivalency of Basic Percents, Fractions, and Decimals • Place Value • Ordering and Comparing Whole Numbers, Fractions, and Decimals • Greater Numbers **Computation:** Addition and Subtraction of Whole Numbers • Multiplication and Division of Whole Numbers • Addition and Subtraction of Simple Fractions with Like and Unlike Denominators • Mixed Numbers and Improper Fractions • Simplest Form • Addition and Subtraction of Decimals • Rounding • Money **Measurement:** Perimeter • Area • Volume • Capacity • Mass • Angle • Circumference • Standard Units • Time **Geometry:** Solids • Plane Figures • Properties of Figures • Congruent or Similar • Transformations • Lines, Rays, Segments, and Angles Statistics and Data Analysis: Mean, Median, and Mode • Graphs, Plots, and Charts Probability: Outcomes and Predictions **Algebra:** Patterns and Rules • Variables • Equations • Expressions • Open Sentences • Coordinate System • Word Problems

McRel Compendium of Content Standards and Skills Index

Content Area	Standards Covered	Specific Skills Covered
Science	• Understands atmospheric processes and the water cycle. • Understands Earth's composition and structure. • Understands the composition and structure of the universe. • Understands the principals of heredity and related concepts. • Understands the structure and function of cells and organisms. • Understands the relationship among organisms and their physical environments. • Understands biological evolution and the diversity of life. • Understands the structure and properties of matter. • Understands the sources and properties of energy. • Understands forces and motion. • Understands the nature of scientific inquiry. • Understands the scientific enterprise.	Animals • Earth • Ecosystems • Electricity and Magnetism • Human Body • Matter • Oceans • Plants • Solar System • Weather
Geography	• The World in Spatial Terms • Places and Regions • Physical Systems • Human Systems • Environment and Society • Uses of Geography	Maps and Globes
History	• Living and Working Together in Families and Communities, Now and Long Ago • The History of the United States: Democratic Principals and Values and the People from Many Cultures who Contributed to its Cultural, Economic, and Political Heritage • The History of Peoples of Many Cultures Around the World	Citizenship • Government

General Test-Taking Strategies

A student's performance on a standardized test is influenced by many things—some are obvious, while others are elusive. Also, there are many factors over which educators have control, while there are many others over which they do not. Until someone invents a magic wand, word, or potion that can be waved over, said to, or imbibed by students, educators will have to rely on more conventional methods to help their students succeed on standardized tests. Below is a list of some general test-taking guidelines with which students should be familiar.

1. Get a good night's sleep the night before the test. Most people need about eight hours.
2. Avoid caffeinated or sugary drinks before taking the test, as they can make you jittery.
3. Eat a well-balanced meal.
4. Wear comfortable clothing.
5. Read or listen to the directions carefully. If something is unclear, ask for clarification.
6. Wear a watch and budget your time.
7. Find out the rules of the test. Will you be penalized for answering something incorrectly? For leaving something blank? Will partial credit be given?
8. If you get stuck on a question, mark it and move on. You can come back to it later.
9. If the test permits, do a memory check. Jot down important formulas or information on a piece of scrap paper.
10. Use mnemonic devices to jog your memory, such as "never eat soggy waffles" for the four compass points: north, south, east, and west.

Reducing Test Anxiety

Anxiety can be debilitating in a test-taking situation, but it is important to remember that not all students experience test anxiety. There is a story about a first-year teacher who entered his room on test day and said jokingly to his seventh-grade class, "Well, is everybody nervous?" A student raised his hand and replied, "I'm nervous that I'm not nervous!"

Some students experience test anxiety, while others do not. And there are students for whom tests occasion a modicum of anxiety that not only does not inhibit their performance, but actually enhances it! The type of test anxiety we are concerned with here is the kind that severely impedes a student's ability to perform on a standardized test. But how do you know when a student has this kind of anxiety? There are several things that might tip you off:

- Tardiness on test day
- Absenteeism on test day
- Crying
- Hyperactivity
- Lethargy
- Jitteriness

- Shallow breathing
- Sweating
- Distractibility/inability to focus/going blank
- Nausea
- Muscle tension

Of course, one of the biggest clues of test anxiety is when a student who demonstrates knowledge and understanding of content via his/her daily classroom performance falls apart when confronted with a standardized test which is assessing the same skills.

Fortunately, there are a variety of strategies that can be taught to students suffering from test anxiety that can help them manage it. These strategies, however, should be routinely practiced by students in order for them to be effective. There is very little point in modeling positive self-talk five minutes before a test and then expecting that it will be of any use.

A Note to the Test Givers

Students are not the only people who experience test anxiety. Teachers, administrators, and other school personnel responsible for administering standardized tests can also experience anxiety around test time as pressure to increase student achievement mounts. While this is understandable, it is important to remember that anxiety is contagious: Anxious educators can often, inadvertently, create anxious students. Be mindful of your demeanor when administering the test. Create a relaxed, positive environment. Smile and maintain your sense of humor. Know that you have done your best to prepare your students. And your best is all you and they can do!

Strategies for Reducing Test Anxiety

The following pages contain some of the most effective strategies available to help elementary, middle, high school, and even college students overcome test anxiety. By familiarizing students with all of these strategies, and providing opportunities for them to practice, students will be better able to determine not only which strategies they are most comfortable using, but which strategies have the greatest impact on reducing their test anxiety.

✓ **Positive Self-Talk**

Anxiety and negativity are akin to the old chicken and egg situation: Does our anxiety cause us to make negative statements to ourselves or do our negative self-statements create the anxiety? Let's just say that test anxiety and negative self-talk are inextricably linked—if you find an anxious student, you will probably also find a student who is telling him/herself that he/she is going to fail. Positive self-talk consists of simple positive, yet realistic, statements and repeating these statements to oneself in an anxiety-provoking situation. Some examples of positive self-talk are:

➢ I can do this.

➢ I know this material.

➢ I have practiced this material.

➢ I'm intelligent.

The trick to using this strategy is for students to keep the statements simple and to have them practice using them prior to any test-taking situation. You don't want them to have to come up with the statements at the moment they are confronted with the test!

✓ **Visualization**

There are essentially two types of creative visualization that can be used to help combat test anxiety. Let us call the first type the *Safe Place Method*, which requires students to conjure a mental image of a place, either real or imagined, that is both relaxing and safe. Provide students with the following instructions in order to practice this method:

➢ Close your eyes.

➢ Calm your breath.

➢ Picture your safe place.

➢ Look up and down and to the left and to the right of your safe place.

➢ Take notice of what you see, smell, and feel.

➢ Smile.

✓ **Visualization** *(cont.)*

The second visualization technique we will call the *Olympic Method*. This method, often used by athletes, requires that individuals imagine what they are trying to achieve, whether it be crossing the finish line first, hitting a home run, or acing a test! Have students practice the following steps:

➤ Close your eyes.

➤ Calm your breath.

➤ Picture yourself confidently taking the test.

➤ Remember another test in which you did well.

➤ Imagine yourself receiving a high test score or grade.

➤ Smile.

✓ **Progressive Muscle Relaxation**

Anxiety has both a psychological and physiological component. Muscle tension is a common response to test anxiety that can be minimized by using progressive muscle relaxation. This method involves focusing on and then tensing and relaxing large muscle groups in a particular order.

➤ Begin at your toes. Tighten or clench your toes and hold for three to five seconds. Release.

➤ Move upward to your feet, calves, thighs, and so forth. Tighten each muscle group for five seconds, then release.

➤ Once you have moved through your body, take a few deep breaths.

✓ **Controlled Breathing**

It is a rare person indeed who has never experienced shallow breathing when in an anxiety-filled situation. In fact, shallow, short breaths are a universal indicator of someone who is overwhelmed by anxiety. Practicing controlled breathing is a simple, yet powerful, way in which to deal with all kinds of anxiety.

➤ Sit comfortably.

➤ Place your hand on your stomach.

➤ Breathe gently in through your nose for a count of four.

➤ Let your breath expand your belly. Observe your stomach rising.

➤ Breathe out for a count of four.

➤ Observe your stomach flattening.

➤ Repeat.

No doubt you will have noticed that all of the aforementioned techniques have to do with changing what we say, what we see, and what we feel. The mind and the body are woven tightly together like a carpet, and often all one needs to do to unravel the pattern of test anxiety woven into the fabric is to pull on one tiny thread. In order for these strategies to be successful, however, students must routinely practice them, especially in non-test-taking situations.

Familiarity and proficiency with these methods will empower students and give them the extra tools they need to do their best.

Multiple-Choice Questions

Whether your school or district administers the Iowa Test of Basic Skills, the Terra Nova Achievement Test, or the Texas Assessment of Knowledge and Skills, the vast majority of test questions that students will encounter will be in a multiple-choice format. For this reason, it's important for students to understand not only how these types of questions are constructed and what they are trying to assess, but also what general strategies they can apply to help them arrive at the correct answers.

All multiple-choice questions contain a *stem*, or incomplete statement, and four to five choices. Only one of the choices is the correct answer, and the others are called decoys, or *distractors*. The purpose of a multiple-choice question is to determine whether students can tease out the correct information when it is surrounded by incorrect information. For example:

The Declaration of Independence was written by *(stem)*

Ⓐ **Jefferson Davis.**   (*distractor*)

Ⓑ **Thomas Jefferson.**   (*correct option*)

Ⓒ **Jefferson Airplane.**   (*distractor*)

Ⓓ **George Jefferson.**   (*distractor*)

Ⓔ **All of the above**   (*distractor*)

Extreme Words and Statements

Extreme words and statements, like extreme sports, can be dangerous . . . especially on standardized tests. Take, if you will, this rather extreme statement:

I always eat healthy foods.

Ah, if only it were true! The fact is that the word *always* makes this statement extreme and, therefore, very likely to be false. It's not only important for students to understand how words can affect the veracity of statements, but also how to recognize and navigate qualifiers and absolutes in both stems and options.

Absolutes are words such as *always, never, all, none,* and *only.* Words like these tend to make statements false. Because multiple-choice questions often require students to create true statements, by combining stems and options, absolute words, when encountered on standardized tests, should ring the alarm. There are very few things in life for which there are no exceptions. Absolute words close all doors and windows. They do not allow for the possibility of something occurring even once.

Qualifiers are words such as *many, often, some, rarely,* and *may.* These kinds of words tend to make statements true, and when they appear in options could indicate the correct answer. Unlike absolutes, qualifiers leave the door ajar and the window slightly cracked. They allow for the possibility of something occurring even if it only happens once in a blue moon. Try this one with your class:

The class of animals known as mammals

Ⓐ **never lay eggs.**   (*absolute*)

Ⓑ **always lay eggs.**   (*absolute*)

Ⓒ **rarely lay eggs.**   (*qualifier*)

Ⓓ **None of the above**

Here we have two options in which there are absolute words and one in which there is a qualifier. Now let's try to create some true statements.

   a. **It is true that the class of animals known as mammals never lay eggs.**

   b. **It is true that the class of animals known as mammals always lay eggs.**

   c. **It is true that the class of animals known as mammals rarely lay eggs.**

In order for either *a* or *b* to be correct, it would mean that either there are no mammals, anywhere on the face of the earth, that lay eggs or that all mammals, without exception, lay eggs. Both of these options are extreme and, therefore, likely to be false. While most mammals give birth to live young, there are a few who do indeed lay eggs, such as the duck-billed platypus and the echidna.

Meta-Multiple Choice

Following are several strategies that students can use when confronted by multiple-choice questions and a practice multiple-choice test. The purpose of this test is not to assess content knowledge, but to provide students with an opportunity to both ponder and practice applying these strategies. Copy and distribute pages 13 through 15. Students can work individually, in pairs, or in a larger group. Encourage students to identify which strategies they used and what clues contained within the stems or the options helped them to arrive at the correct answers. Before students begin, it will be important to remind them that these strategies are guidelines and should not be applied thoughtlessly.

The Secrets to Acing Tests!

When we teach our students test-taking strategies, we run the risk of inadvertently implying that it is possible to do well on a test by simply strategizing alone. This, of course, is not the case. No test-taking strategy can take the place of simply knowing the material, and it is important that this be stated explicitly to students. Students who understand the material and who are confident usually don't need strategies to help them do well on tests; and if they do, it is only on about ten percent of the test items. It is critical that teachers share the most important and foolproof test-taking strategies that exist with their students.

The Secrets to Acing Tests!

✓ Attend school regularly and be on time.

✓ Come to school prepared, rested, and ready to learn.

✓ Complete all of your classroom and homework assignments.

✓ Ask for help if you don't understand.

✓ Spend time every day studying and reviewing material.

✓ Create an organized and quiet place in which to study.

✓ Know that procrastination is the enemy of achievement.

Multiple-Choice Strategies

1. Read the stem carefully.

2. Cover the options and make a prediction.

3. If your prediction or something close to it appears, select it.

4. If your prediction does not appear, read each option carefully.

5. Eliminate any silly options.

6. Eliminate any options you know to be incorrect.

7. A stem and option that creates a grammatically incorrect statement may be an indication that it is wrong.

8. Preface the stem and option choice with the phrase "It is true that. . ." If the stem and option creates a true statement, it is an indication that it is correct.

9. If "All of the above" is an option and at least two of the other options are correct, then select "All of the above."

10. If "All of the above" is an option and you know that at least one of the options is wrong, then eliminate both "All of the above" and the other incorrect option.

11. If "None of the above" is an option and at least one of the options is correct, then eliminate "None of the above" as a possibility.

Multiple-Choice Practice Questions

Directions: Using the strategies you have learned so far, fill in the answer circles for your choices. After you have answered each question, write down which strategy you used and explain why you used it.

1. Lewis and Clark were
   - Ⓐ a famous comedy team.
   - Ⓑ American explorers.
   - Ⓒ English explorers.
   - Ⓓ generals during the American Revolution.

THINK! Which strategy did you use and why?

2. A word of opposite meaning is
   - Ⓔ a synonym.
   - Ⓕ a homonym.
   - Ⓖ an antonym.
   - Ⓗ a metaphor.

THINK! Which strategy did you use and why?

3. Which is a region of the United States?
   - Ⓐ Northeast
   - Ⓑ Southeast
   - Ⓒ Midwest
   - Ⓓ West
   - Ⓔ All of the above

THINK! Which strategy did you use and why?

4. The term *author's point of view* refers to
   - Ⓕ what the author is looking at when he/she writes the story.
   - Ⓖ the author's opinion.
   - Ⓗ the title of the story.
   - Ⓘ the characters in the story.

THINK! Which strategy did you use and why?

5.   A polygon is

   (A)   a line segment.

   (B)   a sphere.

   (C)   another name for a square.

   (D)   a closed plane figure composed of straight lines.

THINK! Which strategy did you use and why?

---

6.   The sentence "An apple a day keeps the doctor away," most likely means that

   (E)   doctors are afraid of apples.

   (F)   eating healthy foods helps keep you healthy.

   (G)   doctors refuse to treat patients who eat apples.

   (H)   if you eat apples you will never get sick.

THINK! Which strategy did you use and why?

---

7.   The shell of an oyster or clam can also be called

   (A)   skin.

   (B)   an exoskeleton.

   (C)   a membrane.

   (D)   a vertebra.

THINK! Which strategy did you use and why?

---

8.   A quotient is produced by

   (E)   multiplying the factors.

   (F)   adding the addends.

   (G)   dividing the dividend by the divisor.

   (H)   subtracting the numerators.

   (I)   None of the above

THINK! Which strategy did you use and why?

More Multiple-Choice Practice

Now that students have some familiarity with the ins and outs of multiple-choice questions, have them participate in the activity described below.

Test Takers to Test Makers!

Students are frequently cast in the role as test takers, but how often do they get to be the test makers? To help students internalize the multiple-choice strategies they have learned, have them participate in the following activity:

- Either in pairs or individually, have students select a content area with which they feel comfortable.
- Ask them to create ten multiple-choice questions based on current classroom learning.
- Tell them that each question must contain a stem and four to five options.
- The options must contain one correct answer and several distracters.
- The distracters should include some of the errors previously discussed.
- When tests are completed, have students swap with each other to not only take the test, but to also practice using the various multiple-choice strategies and identifying various types of errors.

Getting to Know Test Structure

While the element of surprise is great when it comes to a pun, plot, or party, it can be the proverbial kiss of death when it comes to a standardized test! Standardized tests come in particular forms, and just as it is important for students to know the content they may encounter and the strategies that they can use, they will also need to become familiar with the physicality of the test itself. In other words, they should be familiar with how the test is organized, how to mark their answers, and when and where to stop throughout the test. To increase the odds of students doing their best, make sure that they understand the following:

Remember...

- Standardized tests are given to thousands of students and are marked or graded by a computer. The computer will not interpret your answer the way your teacher might. It will either mark an answer right or wrong.
- Fill in each bubble completely and stay within the lines.
- If you need to erase, do so completely.
- Do not make any stray marks on the test sheet. Use scrap paper to work out problems or jot down ideas.
- Make sure that the answer you mark corresponds to the question being asked.
- Look for the words STOP and GO in the lower right-hand corner of test pages. These words will indicate whether or not you are finished or if there are more pages to complete.

Marking Your Answers

The purpose of this lesson is to introduce you to the correct way to mark your answers on a standardized test.

A standardized test is one that is given to thousands and thousands of students. The writers of the questions try to be as fair as possible. After all, it wouldn't mean anything if all fourth-grade students took different kinds of tests—some easy, some hard. The results would be confusing and meaningless.

The scoring of standardized tests tries to be as fair as possible, too. It is done by a computer. However, for computer-scored tests, answer sheets must be marked the same way by all students. That is why everyone must use a pencil marked No. 2 and fill in the circles with dark marks.

Attention must also be paid to how a question is written. For example, a question on a standardized test might look like this:

Directions: Fill in the answer circle for your choice.

How do you write the plural of the word *mouse*?

mouses	mices	mice	meeses
○	○	○	○

You would fill in the circle below *mice*. But what if the question were written this way?

Directions: Fill in the answer circle for your choice.

How do you write the plural of *house*?

Ⓐ hice
Ⓑ hices
Ⓒ hoose
Ⓓ houses

You would fill in the circle with D inside of it, not just fill in the D before the word *houses*. If you did that, the computer would mark your answer as incorrect. Unfortunately, the computer would have no way of determining that you knew the plural of house!

Marking Your Answers *(cont.)*

Of course, you will not fill in answers as soon as you are handed a standardized test. The first thing you will do is put your name on the answer sheet. Here is an example:

Each filled-in circle stands for a letter in someone's name. Figure out the person's name by looking at the filled-in circles and then writing the letter of the circle in the empty box above the row. Notice that the person filled in blank circles for spaces anywhere in her name, including leftover spaces at the end. Circles must be filled in under every box.

Did you figure out the person's name?

Last Name

First Name

Reading Comprehension Tests: Literal, Inferential, and Analytical Questions

Standardized tests will always require students to navigate a reading comprehension section in order to assess their reading ability, and it is probably this part of any standardized test that strikes the most fear into the hearts and minds of educators. That is because we know that reading is not only difficult to teach, but also difficult to learn, and that the ability for a student to truly comprehend what they have read depends upon them mastering a complex set of skills. So let's be clear. There is no strategy that can help a poor reader do well on a standardized test. The strategies we will speak of here are intended to be useful to those students who read at or above their grade level.

One of the most effective things you can do for your students is to clue them into the types of questions they will encounter on a reading comprehension test. The elimination of the element of surprise will go a long way in helping your students do their best.

Reading comprehension tests usually contain literal, inferential, and analytical questions about both fiction and nonfiction passages.

- **Literal Questions:** These kinds of questions require you to recall or locate a detail which appears in the passage. The best strategy to use here is to simply go back to the passage and find the information.

- **Inferential Questions:** These kinds of questions require you to make a deduction, to read between the lines of a passage, or to look for information that may be unstated. To answer these types of questions, you have to use clues from the passage along with what you know in order to arrive at the correct answer.

- **Analytical Questions:** These types of questions require you to rely more on your own experience than the passage itself in order to arrive at the correct answer. Analytical questions often involve examining the author's purpose or point of view.

Use the following story and practice test during whole-group instruction. Have students practice answering reading comprehension questions and identifying the types of question being posed.

Practice Comprehension Questions

Mercury and the Woodman

By Aesop

A woodman was chopping down a tree on the bank of a river. His axe accidentally flew out of his hands and fell into the water. The woodman was upset that he lost his axe. Suddenly, Mercury appeared and asked him why he was so upset. The woodman told Mercury what happened. Mercury felt sorry for the man so he dove into the river and brought up a golden axe. He asked the woodman if this was the one he had lost. The woodman said that it was not. Mercury dove a second time and brought up a silver axe. He asked the woodman if this was his axe. "No, that is not mine either," said the woodman. Once more Mercury dove into the river and brought up the missing axe. The woodman was happy at getting his axe back. He thanked Mercury warmly. Mercury was so pleased with his honesty that he gave him the other two axes.

When the woodman told the story to his friends, one of them became jealous. He decided to try his luck for himself. So he went and began to chop a tree at the edge of the river. He let his axe drop into the water on purpose. Mercury appeared as before. When he found out that the man's axe fell in the river, he dove in and brought up a golden axe. The fellow cried, "That's mine. That's mine." He reached out his hand for the prize. Mercury was so disgusted at his dishonesty that he refused to give him the golden axe. He also refused to get the axe that he let fall into the stream.

Directions: Read each question and fill in the answer circle for your choice. After you have answered each question, think about whether the question is *literal*, *inferential*, or *analytical*.

1. How did the woodman lose his axe?

   Ⓐ He threw it away because it was broken.

   Ⓑ It accidentally flew out of his hand.

   Ⓒ His jealous friend stole it from him.

   Ⓓ Mercury stole it from him.

THINK! What kind of question is this?

---

2. Mercury decides to help the woodman because

   Ⓔ he loves him.

   Ⓕ he owes him a favor.

   Ⓖ he feels sorry for him.

   Ⓗ he promised him that he would.

THINK! What kind of question is this?

---

3. Why do you think Mercury helps the woodman?

    Ⓐ He's bored.

    Ⓑ He's trying to impress him.

    Ⓒ He's trying to win favor with the other gods.

    Ⓓ He sees that the woodman is a humble, hardworking man.

THINK! What kind of question is this?

---

4. What is the second axe that Mercury retrieves made of?

    Ⓔ silver

    Ⓕ gold

    Ⓖ wood

    Ⓗ bronze

THINK! What kind of a question is this?

---

5. Why is producing a gold and silver axe a good way to determine if the woodman is honest?

    Ⓐ Woodmen love axes.

    Ⓑ Woodmen rely on axes for their living.

    Ⓒ People are often tempted by great wealth.

    Ⓓ None of the above

THINK! What kind of a question is this?

The Organization of Fiction and Nonfiction

Another good strategy with which students should be familiar is remembering how both fiction and nonfiction are organized. This will help them when they are confronted by questions that ask them to locate main ideas, problems, solutions, and supporting details. By the intermediate and middle school grades, most students have internalized this structure, so here we are simply reminding them of what they already know.

Fiction:

- **The Beginning:** In most works of fiction, information about the main characters and setting comes at the beginning of the story.

- **The Middle:** In most works of fiction, information about the problem that the characters are trying to solve comes in the middle of the story.

- **The End:** In most works of fiction, information about how the characters solve their problems comes at the end of the story.

Nonfiction:

- **The Beginning:** In most works of nonfiction, the main idea (and topic sentence) can be found at the beginning of the selection.

- **The Middle:** In most works of nonfiction, elaboration of the main idea, in the form of supporting details, can be found in the middle of the selection.

- **The End:** In most works of nonfiction, a summary of the main idea can be found at the end of the selection.

Use the following fiction and nonfiction passages and practice tests during whole-group instruction. Have students practice answering reading comprehension questions and encourage them to justify their answers.

The Pied Piper

Adapted by the Brothers Grimm

In Upper Saxony there is a town called Hamelin. It is located in the region of Kalenberg. Hamlin is located right where two large rivers join together.

In the year of 1384, this town was infested by so many rats that they ate all of the corn the people had been storing for the winter months. They tried everything to chase away the rats, but nothing worked. One day a stranger came to town. He was taller than most men. He wore colorful clothes. He told the townspeople that he could get rid of the rats if they would pay him a fee. The townspeople agreed.

The stranger took a flute from his jacket. As soon as he started to play all of the rats came out of their holes and followed him. The stranger led them straight to the river. The rats ran into the river and were drowned. When he returned he asked for his money. They townspeople refused to pay. The next day there was a fair in the town. The stranger waited for the older townspeople to go to church. He took out another flute and began to play a song. All the boys in town above the age of fourteen gathered around him. He led them to the neighboring mountain, named Kopfelberg. Underneath this mountain is a sewer for the town. It is also where criminals are executed. All of the boys disappeared and were never seen again. A young girl who was following them saw what happened and brought the news of it to the town.

Directions: Read the passage and then fill in the answer circles for your choices. Think about how you know which is the correct answer.

1. Where is this story set?
   - Ⓐ Kopfelberg Mountain
   - Ⓑ The town of Hamelin
   - Ⓒ Weser
   - Ⓓ Hamel

THINK! How do you know?

2. Who is the main character in this story?
   - Ⓔ a young girl
   - Ⓕ the narrator
   - Ⓖ the Pied Piper
   - Ⓗ the boys

THINK! How do you know?

3. The Pied Piper is described as being
   - Ⓐ shorter than most men.
   - Ⓑ rather plump.
   - Ⓒ very devious.
   - Ⓓ taller than most men.

THINK! How do you know?

(GO)

4. What problem does the Pied Piper agree to solve?
   - Ⓔ To rid the town of the rats.
   - Ⓕ To play the flute at festivals.
   - Ⓖ To discipline the badly behaved boys.
   - Ⓗ He doesn't agree to do anything.

THINK! How do you know?

5. How does the Pied Piper drown the rats?
   - Ⓐ He chases them into the water.
   - Ⓑ He lures them to the water.
   - Ⓒ He sets traps along the river.
   - Ⓓ He gathers them up in a sack.

THINK! How do you know?

6. What part do the townspeople play in the disappearance of the boys?
   - Ⓔ They round them up and take them away.
   - Ⓕ They refuse to pay the Pied Piper.
   - Ⓖ They have nothing to do with it.
   - Ⓗ They give the Pied Piper permission to take them away.

THINK! How do you know?

7. It is likely that the rats and the boys followed the Pied Piper because
   - Ⓐ they were not very bright.
   - Ⓑ they liked him.
   - Ⓒ he promised them something.
   - Ⓓ he had magical powers.

THINK! How do you know?

8. The theme of this story is
   - Ⓔ don't trust strangers.
   - Ⓕ honor your debts.
   - Ⓖ don't live in a town with rats.
   - Ⓗ don't listen to flute music.

THINK! How do you know?

Earthquakes

The ground shakes when the crust of the earth moves. This is called an earthquake. It can be caused by the crust sliding, volcanic bursts, or man-made explosions. Earthquakes that cause the most damage come from the crust sliding.

At first, the crust may only bend because of pushing forces. But when the pushing becomes too much, the crust snaps and shifts into a new position. Shifting makes wiggles of energy that go out in all directions, like ripples when a stone is dropped in water. These are called *seismic waves*, which travel out from where the center of the earthquake is located. Sometimes people can hear these waves, because they make the whole planet ring like a bell. It must be awesome to hear this sound!

The crust moving may leave a crack, or *fault*, in the land. Geologists, scientists who study the earth's surface, say that earthquakes often happen where there are old faults. There are weak places in the crust. Where there are faults, earthquakes may happen again and again.

Sometimes, when earthquakes happen under the ocean floor, they cause huge sea waves. These waves are called *tsunamis*, which can travel across the ocean as fast as 598 miles per hour and produce waves over 49 feet high. During the 1964 Alaskan earthquake, giant waves caused most of the damage to the towns of Kodiak, Cordova, and Seward. Some waves raced across the ocean in the other direction to the coasts of Japan.

Although earthquakes are usually frightening, keep in mind that the distance to the center of the earth is 3,960 miles. Most earthquakes begin less than 150 miles below the surface. Earthquakes are not a sign that the earth is unsteady.

Directions: Read the passage and then fill in the answer circles for your choices. Think about how you know which is the correct answer.

1. Earthquakes are caused by
   Ⓐ a giant sound beneath the ground.
   Ⓑ explosions and the crust sliding.
   Ⓒ volcanoes.
   Ⓓ B and C.
   Ⓔ none of the above.

THINK! How do you know?

2. Huge waves that rush across the ocean can be caused by
   Ⓕ tsunamis.
   Ⓖ storms.
   Ⓗ earthquakes beneath the ocean.
   Ⓘ waves as high as 49 feet.

THINK! How do you know?

3. Seismic waves are compared to
   Ⓐ ripples in water.
   Ⓑ a bell ringing.
   Ⓒ faults in the ground.
   Ⓓ None of the above

THINK! How do you know?

4. An effect of earthquakes is
   - Ⓔ faults or cracks in the ground.
   - Ⓕ pushing forces building up.
   - Ⓖ an unsteady planet.
   - Ⓗ a stone dropped in the water.

THINK! How do you know?

5. The author's purpose in this passage is
   - Ⓐ to scare the reader.
   - Ⓑ to inform the reader.
   - Ⓒ to entertain the reader.
   - Ⓓ to bore the reader.

THINK! How do you know?

6. When earthquakes happen under the ocean floor they sometimes cause
   - Ⓔ tidal waves.
   - Ⓕ jet streams.
   - Ⓖ tsunamis.
   - Ⓗ None of the above

THINK! How do you know?

7. You read in the newspaper that an old fault has been discovered nearby. What might happen?
   - Ⓐ It will swallow you alive.
   - Ⓑ An earthquake might happen there.
   - Ⓒ A flood might happen there.
   - Ⓓ Not a thing.

THINK! How do you know?

8. An appropriate title for this passage might be
   - Ⓔ When Earthquakes Attack!
   - Ⓕ Giant Waves from Nowhere
   - Ⓖ How Earthquakes Happen
   - Ⓗ The Mysteries of Our Earth

THINK! How do you know?

Syllabication Practice Test 1

Directions: Fill in the answer circle which shows the correct way to divide the word into syllables.

Samples

A. Ⓐ ch-ap-ter

    Ⓑ chap-ter

    Ⓒ cha-pter

B. **Ⓓ cli-mate**

    Ⓔ clim-ate

    Ⓕ cl-im-ate

1. Ⓐ music-ian

    Ⓑ mus-ic-ian

    Ⓒ mu-si-cian

2. Ⓓ fi-ni-sh

    Ⓔ fin-ish

    Ⓕ fini-sh

3. Ⓐ glac-ier

    Ⓑ gla-c-ier

    Ⓒ gla-cier

4. Ⓓ ugli-er

    Ⓔ ug-li-er

    Ⓕ ugl-ier

5. Ⓐ lan-guage

    Ⓑ lan-gu-age

    Ⓒ lang-uage

6. Ⓓ inter-est

    Ⓔ in-ter-est

    Ⓕ int-er-est

7. Ⓐ hour-ly

    Ⓑ ho-ur-ly

    Ⓒ hou-rly

8. Ⓓ pop-ula-tion

    Ⓔ pop-u-la-tion

    Ⓕ pop-u-lat-ion

9. Ⓐ exi-st

    Ⓑ ex-i-st

    Ⓒ ex-ist

10. Ⓓ shag-gy

    Ⓔ sh-ag-gy

    Ⓕ sha-ggy

11. Ⓐ vo-lu-me

    Ⓑ vol-ume

    Ⓒ vol-u-me

12. Ⓓ geo-graphy

    Ⓔ geo-gra-phy

    Ⓕ ge-og-ra-phy

STOP

Syllabication Practice Test 2

Directions: Fill in the answer circle which shows the correct way in which to divide the word into syllables.

Samples

A.	Ⓐ **sys-tem**	
	Ⓑ sy-stem	
	Ⓒ sy-st-em	

B.	Ⓓ ill-us-trate	
	Ⓔ **il-lus-trate**	
	Ⓕ ill-ust-rate	

1. Ⓐ hel-i-cop-ter
   Ⓑ he-li-cop-ter
   Ⓒ heli-cop-ter

7. Ⓐ e-vil
   Ⓑ ev-il
   Ⓒ evil

2. Ⓓ u-ni-on
   Ⓔ un-ion
   Ⓕ uni-on

8. Ⓓ pyra-mid
   Ⓔ py-ra-mid
   Ⓕ pyr-a-mid

3. Ⓐ bil-lion
   Ⓑ bill-ion
   Ⓒ bi-lli-on

9. Ⓐ o-pin-ion
   Ⓑ opin-ion
   Ⓒ o-pi-nion

4. Ⓓ summ-arize
   Ⓔ su-mma-rize
   Ⓕ sum-ma-rize

10. Ⓓ o-cto-pus
    Ⓔ oc-to-pus
    Ⓕ octo-pus

5. Ⓐ sto-ma-ch
   Ⓑ stom-ach
   Ⓒ st-om-ach

11. Ⓐ so-lid
    Ⓑ solid
    Ⓒ sol-id

6. Ⓓ hem-i-sphere
   Ⓔ hemi-sphere
   Ⓕ he-mi-sphere

12. Ⓓ au-di-ence
    Ⓔ a-udi-ence
    Ⓕ audi-ence

Syllabication Practice Test 3

Directions: Fill in the answer circle which shows the correct way in which to divide the word into syllables.

A. (A) **hus-band** **Samples** **B.** (D) alpha-be-ti-cal

(B) hu-s-band (E) al-pha-be-tical

(C) hus-ba-nd (F) **al-pha-bet-i-cal**

1. (A) deve-lop 7. (A) can-yon

(B) de-vel-op (B) ca-ny-on

(C) dev-elop (C) cany-on

2. (D) exper-i-ment 8. (D) fina-lly

(E) ex-peri-ment (E) fi-na-lly

(F) ex-per-i-ment (F) fi-nal-ly

3. (A) fam-ous 9. (A) pecsti-cide

(B) fa-mous (B) pe-sti-cide

(C) fam-o-us (C) pes-ti-cide

4. (D) squi-rr-el 10. (D) lab-or

(E) sq-ui-rrel (E) labor

(F) squir-rel (F) la-bor

5. (A) rib-bon 11. (A) pre-vi-ous

(B) ribb-on (B) pre-vious

(C) ri-bbon (C) pre-vio-us

6. (D) mess-en-ger 12. (D) mo-is-ture

(E) mes-sen-ger (E) mois-ture

(F) mess-en-ger (F) moist-ure

Syllabication Practice Test 4

Directions: Fill in the answer circle which shows the correct way in which to divide the word into syllables.

Samples

A.   Ⓐ auto-matic   B.   Ⓓ dis-respect

     Ⓑ auto-ma-tic   Ⓔ **dis-re-spect**

     Ⓒ **au-to-mat-ic**   Ⓕ disre-spect

1.   Ⓐ ro-ya-l
    Ⓑ roy-al
    Ⓒ ro-y-al

2.   Ⓓ un-even
    Ⓔ un-ev-en
    Ⓕ un-e-ven

3.   Ⓐ bar-be-cue
    Ⓑ bar-becue
    Ⓒ barb-e-cue

4.   Ⓓ gu-il-ty
    Ⓔ guilt-y
    Ⓕ guil-ty

5.   Ⓐ act-ivity
    Ⓑ act-i-vity
    Ⓒ ac-tiv-i-ty

6.   Ⓓ bold-ness
    Ⓔ bol-dness
    Ⓕ b-old-ness

7.   Ⓐ ma-gni-fy
    Ⓑ mag-nify
    Ⓒ mag-ni-fy

8.   Ⓓ horizon-tal
    Ⓔ hor-i-zon-tal
    Ⓕ hori-zon-tal

9.   Ⓐ pan-ic
    Ⓑ pa-nic
    Ⓒ p-an-ic

10.   Ⓓ oppor-tun-ity
    Ⓔ opp-or-tu-nity
    Ⓕ op-por-tu-ni-ty

11.   Ⓐ iss-ue
    Ⓑ is-sue
    Ⓒ is-su-e

12.   Ⓓ ca-ve-rn
    Ⓔ cav-ern
    Ⓕ cave-rn

STOP

Homographs Which Sound Different
Practice Test 1

Directions: Read each pair of definitions. Find the word that fits both definitions. Fill in the answer circle for your choice.

Samples

A. <u>to show the way</u> and <u>a metallic element</u>

    Ⓐ proceed   Ⓑ tin   Ⓒ **lead**   Ⓓ load

B. <u>a gift</u> and <u>to show</u>

    Ⓔ **present**   Ⓕ introduce   Ⓖ token   Ⓗ award

---

1. <u>a dry expanse of land</u> and <u>to abandon</u>

    Ⓐ plain   Ⓑ leave   Ⓒ desert   Ⓓ gorge

---

2. <u>unwillingness to comply</u> and <u>trash</u>

    Ⓔ refuse   Ⓕ denial   Ⓖ garbage   Ⓗ waste

---

3. <u>to rip</u> and <u>lubricant for the eyes</u>

    Ⓐ slash   Ⓑ sweat   Ⓒ tear   Ⓓ cut

---

4. <u>type of fish</u> and <u>type of musical instrument</u>

    Ⓔ perch   Ⓕ piccolo   Ⓖ bass   Ⓗ salmon

---

5. <u>near to</u> and <u>to shut</u>

    Ⓐ ajar   Ⓑ adjacent   Ⓒ abate   Ⓓ close

---

6. <u>type of bird</u> and <u>past tense of dive</u>

    Ⓔ dove   Ⓕ dives   Ⓖ dived   Ⓗ daved   **STOP**

Homographs Which Sound Different
Practice Test 2

Directions: Read each pair of definitions. Find the word that fits both definitions. Fill in the answer circle for your choice.

Samples

A. <u>a female hog</u> and <u>to plant seeds</u>

    Ⓐ hag   Ⓑ toil   Ⓒ **sow**   Ⓓ mare

B. <u>to bend at the waist</u> and <u>used with an arrow</u>

    Ⓔ point   Ⓕ **bow**   Ⓖ stoop   Ⓗ notch

---

1. <u>plural of *doe*</u> and <u>third person singular tense of *do*</u>

    Ⓐ deer   Ⓑ do   Ⓒ does   Ⓓ done

---

2. <u>to oppose</u> and <u>a thing</u>

    Ⓔ ornament   Ⓕ object   Ⓖ deny   Ⓗ relic

---

3. <u>circulating air</u> and <u>to wrap something around something else</u>

    Ⓐ wind   Ⓑ current   Ⓒ breeze   Ⓓ coil

---

4. <u>a motorized bike</u> and <u>sulked</u>

    Ⓔ Vespa   Ⓕ moped   Ⓖ brood   Ⓗ buggy

---

5. <u>an injury</u> and <u>to have wrapped something around something else</u>

    Ⓐ wound   Ⓑ bruise   Ⓒ wind   Ⓓ sprain

---

6. <u>very small</u> and <u>an increment of time</u>

    Ⓔ millisecond   Ⓕ minute   Ⓖ minuscule   Ⓗ dwarf

STOP

Homographs Which Sound Alike
Practice Test 3

Directions: Read each pair of definitions. Find the word that fits both definitions. Fill in the answer circle for your choice.

Samples

A. kind of transportation and to make animals obey

   Ⓐ plane   Ⓑ steps   **Ⓒ train**   Ⓓ show

B. a support for a sign and to hang a sign

   Ⓔ bar   **Ⓕ post**   Ⓖ chain   Ⓗ hook

---

1. a place where the dead are buried and serious

   Ⓐ vault   Ⓑ grave   Ⓒ tomb   Ⓓ plot

---

2. tools used to chop and the vertical and horizontal X and Y on a graph

   Ⓔ hatchet   Ⓕ saws   Ⓖ axes   Ⓗ planes

---

3. in a straight line and move a boat with oars

   Ⓐ vertical   Ⓑ array   Ⓒ row   Ⓓ uniform

---

4. at the tip of your finger and used by carpenters

   Ⓔ cuticle   Ⓕ end   Ⓖ nail   Ⓗ clipper

---

5. one who waits calmly and a person under the care of a doctor

   Ⓐ client   Ⓑ endurance   Ⓒ nurse   Ⓓ patient

---

6. the underground part of a plant and to look for something

   Ⓔ root   Ⓕ seek   Ⓖ stem   Ⓗ stamen

STOP

Homographs Which Sound Alike
Practice Test 4

Directions: Read each pair of definitions. Find the word that fits both definitions. Fill in the answer circle for your choice.

Samples

A. to examine closely and a place to read quietly

   Ⓐ observatory   **Ⓑ study**   Ⓒ peer   Ⓓ library

B. weapons and part of the human body

   Ⓔ nuclear   Ⓕ mind   **Ⓖ arms**   Ⓗ tank

---

1. to lead an orchestra and behavior

   Ⓐ conduct   Ⓑ control   Ⓒ perform   Ⓓ manage

---

2. to move forward and money gained from a venture

   Ⓔ profits   Ⓕ capital   Ⓖ proceeds   Ⓗ advance

---

3. the center of a hurricane and used to see with

   Ⓐ light   Ⓑ cloudless   Ⓒ pupil   Ⓓ eye

---

4. a part of an elephant and a part of a car

   Ⓔ hood   Ⓕ trunk   Ⓖ tail   Ⓗ nose

---

5. a tale and the level of a floor in a building

   Ⓐ story   Ⓑ tier   Ⓒ chapter   Ⓓ table

---

6. sound a dog makes and part of a tree

   Ⓔ yelp   Ⓕ whine   Ⓖ leaf   Ⓗ bark

STOP

Affixes Practice Test 1

Directions: Read each pair of words and look for the word or words that best tell the meaning of the underlined affix. Fill in the answer circle for your choice.

Samples

A <u>bi</u>cycle   <u>bi</u>noculars
- Ⓐ away
- Ⓑ not
- **Ⓒ two**
- Ⓓ between

B hero<u>ic</u>   acid<u>ic</u>
- Ⓔ some
- **Ⓕ like**
- Ⓖ in the direction of
- Ⓗ one who

---

1. <u>auto</u>biography   <u>auto</u>mobile
   - Ⓐ alone
   - Ⓑ self
   - Ⓒ one
   - Ⓓ two

2. <u>oct</u>opus   <u>oct</u>agon
   - Ⓔ ten
   - Ⓕ eight
   - Ⓖ many
   - Ⓗ one

3. <u>uni</u>form   <u>uni</u>corn
   - Ⓐ after
   - Ⓑ before
   - Ⓒ one
   - Ⓓ under

4. <u>geo</u>graphy   <u>geo</u>logy
   - Ⓔ air
   - Ⓕ water
   - Ⓖ rocks
   - Ⓗ Earth

5. sing<u>er</u>   danc<u>er</u>
   - Ⓐ able to
   - Ⓑ like
   - Ⓒ with
   - Ⓓ one who

6. <u>mini</u>series   <u>mini</u>skirt
   - Ⓔ large
   - Ⓕ single
   - Ⓖ small
   - Ⓗ all

7. polite<u>ly</u>   rude<u>ly</u>
   - Ⓐ without
   - Ⓑ having the characteristic of
   - Ⓒ after
   - Ⓓ full of

8. photo<u>graphy</u>   carto<u>graphy</u>
   - Ⓔ the study of
   - Ⓕ the love of
   - Ⓖ the dislike of
   - Ⓗ the knowledge of

STOP

Affixes Practice Test 2

Directions: Read each pair of words and look for the word or words that best tell the meaning of the underlined affix. Fill in the answer circle for your choice.

Samples

A. <u>sub</u>merge   <u>sub</u>soil

- Ⓐ across
- **Ⓑ under**
- Ⓒ less
- Ⓓ greater

B. fro<u>zen</u>   wood<u>en</u>

- Ⓔ ablé to
- **Ⓕ made of**
- Ⓖ away from
- Ⓗ with

---

1. thought<u>less</u>   meaning<u>less</u>
   - Ⓐ below
   - Ⓑ without
   - Ⓒ like
   - Ⓓ opposite from

2. <u>out</u>run   <u>out</u>do
   - Ⓔ through
   - Ⓕ less
   - Ⓖ more
   - Ⓗ under

3. <u>over</u>population   <u>over</u>flow
   - Ⓐ too much
   - Ⓑ not enough
   - Ⓒ around
   - Ⓓ through

4. <u>mis</u>behave   <u>mis</u>take
   - Ⓔ all
   - Ⓕ wrong
   - Ⓖ confusing
   - Ⓗ one

5. tear<u>ful</u>   wonder<u>ful</u>
   - Ⓐ without
   - Ⓑ full of
   - Ⓒ feeling of
   - Ⓓ knowing

6. up<u>ward</u>   west<u>ward</u>
   - Ⓔ with speed
   - Ⓕ with caution
   - Ⓖ in the direction of
   - Ⓗ away from

7. <u>centi</u>meter   <u>centi</u>pede
   - Ⓐ ten
   - Ⓑ hundred
   - Ⓒ thousand
   - Ⓓ ten thousand

8. <u>non</u>violence   <u>non</u>sense
   - Ⓔ having
   - Ⓕ belonging to
   - Ⓖ bad
   - Ⓗ not

STOP

Vocabulary

Synonyms and Antonyms
Practice Test 1

Directions: Read each sentence, paying close attention to the underlined word. For sentences 1–5, choose the synonym of the underlined word. For sentences 6–10, choose the antonym of the underlined word.

Samples

Choose the Synonym

A. We had a <u>wonderful</u> time on our vacation.
- (A) sunny
- (B) everyday
- (C) **spectacular**
- (D) common

Choose the Antonym

B. I felt <u>weary</u> after dance practice.
- (E) **alert**
- (F) miserable
- (G) proud
- (H) tired

Choose the Synonym

1. Our bus was <u>delayed</u> one hour.
- (A) held-up
- (B) on-time
- (C) cancelled
- (D) postponed

2. The <u>device</u> was called a telescope.
- (E) plan
- (F) equipment
- (G) microscope
- (H) thing

3. The <u>exterior</u> of the house was red and white.
- (A) inside
- (B) roof
- (C) outside
- (D) backyard

4. My teacher told me that I was <u>tardy</u>.
- (E) on time
- (F) absent
- (G) intelligent
- (H) late

5. After the walk-a-thon we were all <u>fatigued</u>.
- (A) energized
- (B) tired
- (C) cranky
- (D) hungry

Choose the Antonym

6. A <u>majority</u> of the students wanted extra homework.
- (E) fraction
- (F) percentage
- (G) minority
- (H) sampling

7. The cafeteria is <u>adjacent</u> to the library.
- (A) next to
- (B) away from
- (C) perpendicular to
- (D) parallel to

8. The <u>penalty</u> was to sit out the entire game.
- (E) reward
- (F) punishment
- (G) insult
- (H) mistake

9. A river delta is usually very <u>fertile</u> land.
- (A) arable
- (B) dry
- (C) wooded
- (D) barren

10. Measles is a <u>contagious</u> disease.
- (E) transmittable
- (F) noncommunicable
- (G) fatal
- (H) itchy

STOP

Synonyms and Antonyms
Practice Test 2

Directions: Read each sentence, paying close attention to the underlined word. For sentences 1–5, choose the synonym of the underlined word. For sentences 6–10, choose the antonym of the underlined word.

Samples

Choose the Synonym

A. Jermaine was feeling <u>anxious</u> as he waited to make his speech.

   Ⓐ relaxed   Ⓒ brave

   Ⓑ fearful   Ⓓ feverish

Choose the Antonym

B. A heavy frost will <u>spoil</u> the tomatoes that are still outside.

   Ⓐ improve   Ⓒ stop

   Ⓑ soften   Ⓓ rot

Choose the Synonym

1. In order to <u>prevent</u> an accident I wore safety goggles and gloves.

   Ⓐ cause   Ⓒ create

   Ⓑ avoid   Ⓓ remove

2. The average <u>precipitation</u> in my state is 30 inches per year.

   Ⓔ temperature   Ⓖ wind velocity

   Ⓕ humidity   Ⓗ rainfall

3. On Fridays, I <u>deposit</u> my allowance into the bank.

   Ⓐ put   Ⓒ spend

   Ⓑ withdrawal   Ⓓ save

4. The citizens put up a lot of <u>resistance</u> to the mayor's proposal.

   Ⓔ approval   Ⓖ opposition

   Ⓕ willingness   Ⓗ acceptance

5. The punch line to that joke is so <u>obvious</u>!

   Ⓐ meaningless   Ⓒ nonsensical

   Ⓑ apparent   Ⓓ shallow

Choose the Antonym

6. One day I hope to visit many <u>foreign</u> countries.

   Ⓔ domestic   Ⓖ distant

   Ⓕ alien   Ⓗ local

7. Professional athletics are often very <u>wealthy</u>.

   Ⓐ rich   Ⓒ skillfull

   Ⓑ polite   Ⓓ poor

8. The first time I debated I felt a little <u>awkward</u>.

   Ⓔ strange   Ⓖ uneasy

   Ⓕ comfortable   Ⓗ silly

9. My mother says that <u>compassion</u> is a very important quality.

   Ⓐ disregard   Ⓒ acceptance

   Ⓑ kindness   Ⓓ consideration

10. The forecast said to expect a <u>severe</u> snowstorm.

   Ⓔ treacherous   Ⓖ heavy

   Ⓕ mild   Ⓗ blinding

STOP

Similes

Directions: Read each sentence. Look for words or phrases that have the same or almost the same meaning as the underlined phrase. Fill in the answer circle for your choice.

Samples

A. My baby brother <u>eats like a bird</u>.

- Ⓐ eats slowly
- **Ⓑ eats very little**
- Ⓒ eats a lot
- Ⓓ eats really fast

B. The student was <u>as sharp as a tack</u>.

- Ⓔ mean
- Ⓕ funny
- **Ⓖ smart**
- Ⓗ goofy

---

1. She crossed the finish line <u>like greased lightning</u>.

   - Ⓐ clumsily
   - Ⓑ happily
   - Ⓒ quickly
   - Ⓓ slowly

2. The basketball team <u>worked like dogs</u> to prepare for the championship game.

   - Ⓔ worked hard
   - Ⓕ were unorganized
   - Ⓖ were arguing
   - Ⓗ were enjoying themselves

3. The answer to this question is as <u>plain as day</u>.

   - Ⓐ very subtle
   - Ⓑ very difficult
   - Ⓒ very obvious
   - Ⓓ very easy

4. After hockey practice I was <u>sweating like a pig</u>.

   - Ⓔ sweating a lot
   - Ⓕ sweating very little
   - Ⓖ only sweating around the face and head
   - Ⓗ only sweating on the back

5. Juan said that he felt <u>like a fish out of water</u> at this new school.

   - Ⓐ comfortable
   - Ⓑ confident
   - Ⓒ uncomfortable
   - Ⓓ frightened

6. He was running around <u>like a chicken with its head cut off</u>.

   - Ⓔ frantically
   - Ⓕ awkwardly
   - Ⓖ nervously
   - Ⓗ quickly

7. We are <u>like night and day</u>.

   - Ⓐ similar
   - Ⓑ look alike
   - Ⓒ different
   - Ⓓ happy and sad

8. The toddler ran around the grocery store <u>like a bull in a china shop</u>.

   - Ⓔ gracefully
   - Ⓕ happily
   - Ⓖ carefully
   - Ⓗ clumsily

Idioms

Directions: Read each sentence. Look for words or phrases that have the same or almost the same meaning as the underlined phrase. Fill in the answer circle for your choice.

Samples

A. Carlos thinks that ghost stories are a bunch of <u>mumbo jumbo</u>.

Ⓐ **nonsense**
Ⓑ bad luck
Ⓒ proof
Ⓓ doubletalk

B. Shelly told her little brother to <u>put a sock in it</u>.

Ⓔ clean up his room
Ⓕ tell a joke
Ⓖ **be quiet**
Ⓗ start talking

---

1. The mini-mart is open <u>twenty-four seven</u>.

   Ⓐ seven days a week and twenty-four hours a day
   Ⓑ seven days a week
   Ⓒ five days a week twenty-four hours a day
   Ⓓ closed on holidays

2. After we lost the game our coach told us to <u>keep our chins up</u>.

   Ⓔ feel embarrased
   Ⓕ practice more
   Ⓖ apologize to him
   Ⓗ don't get discouraged

3. After football practice we were all ready to <u>chow down</u>.

   Ⓐ take a nap
   Ⓑ wash our dirty clothes
   Ⓒ eat
   Ⓓ take a shower

4. The lunchroom attendant told the students to <u>hold their horses</u>.

   Ⓔ get their money ready
   Ⓕ get in a straight line
   Ⓖ sit down quietly
   Ⓗ be patient

5. Kelly said, "I can't go to the movies tonight, but <u>I'll give you a rain check</u>."

   Ⓐ a call
   Ⓑ go another time
   Ⓒ pay your way
   Ⓓ None of the above

6. Our teacher said he was feeling a little <u>under the weather</u>.

   Ⓔ sad
   Ⓕ happy
   Ⓖ angry
   Ⓗ sick

7. My father told my sister and me to <u>shake a leg</u>.

   Ⓐ hurry up
   Ⓑ slow down
   Ⓒ walk the dog
   Ⓓ do our homework

8. In order to succeed you have to <u>go the extra mile</u>.

   Ⓔ exercise
   Ⓕ go for a long run
   Ⓖ put in extra effort
   Ⓗ be polite

Figurative Language

Fill in the answer circle which tells of what each sentence is an example.

Samples

A. Peter Piper picked a peck of pickled peppers.
- Ⓐ personification
- **Ⓑ alliteration**
- Ⓒ metaphor
- Ⓓ hyperbole

B The birds began to chirp first thing in the morning.
- Ⓔ simile
- Ⓕ idiom
- **Ⓖ onomatopoeia**
- Ⓗ hyperbole

---

1. The rabbit walked into the grocery store and asked for a pound of carrots.
   - Ⓐ personification
   - Ⓑ metaphor
   - Ⓒ alliteration
   - Ⓓ simile

2. Mean monsters munched marshmallows.
   - Ⓔ metaphor
   - Ⓕ idiom
   - Ⓖ onomatopoeia
   - Ⓗ alliteration

3. Man is to boy as woman is to girl.
   - Ⓐ hyperbole
   - Ⓑ analogy
   - Ⓒ simile
   - Ⓓ metaphor

4. I'm so hungry I could eat a horse!
   - Ⓔ personification
   - Ⓕ alliteration
   - Ⓖ hyperbole
   - Ⓗ simile

5. "No man is an island."
   - Ⓐ hyperbole
   - Ⓑ metaphor
   - Ⓒ onamatopoeia
   - Ⓓ idiom

6. Food is to people as gas is to a car.
   - Ⓔ analogy
   - Ⓕ alliteration
   - Ⓖ hyperbole
   - Ⓗ metaphor

7. The sun's rays smiled down upon the earth.
   - Ⓐ personification
   - Ⓑ idiom
   - Ⓒ metaphor
   - Ⓓ analogy

8. The dry leaves rustled in the cool autumn breeze.
   - Ⓔ simile
   - Ⓕ onomatopoeia
   - Ⓖ analogy
   - Ⓗ idiom

Fiction

Directions: Read each passage and then fill in the answer circle for your choice.

Sample

A. Once upon a time, a long time ago, there lived an unhappy king.
This sentence would most likely be found in a

Ⓐ nonfiction book.

Ⓑ autobiography.

Ⓒ **fairy tale.**

Ⓓ poem.

---

1. I was born in a small town in the middle of Pennsylvania.

This sentence would most likely be found in a

Ⓐ biography.

Ⓑ autobiography.

Ⓒ fable.

Ⓓ myth.

---

2. John Henry held up his hammers in victory as the other men shouted and cheered!

This sentence would most likely be found in a

Ⓔ fairy tale.

Ⓕ folktale.

Ⓖ fable.

Ⓗ biography.

---

3. Pandora was very curious about what was inside of the box, so one day she stole the key and opened it.

This sentence would most likely be found in

Ⓐ a myth.

Ⓑ a fable.

Ⓒ nonfiction text.

Ⓓ none of the above.

---

4. Booker T. Washington was one of the most influential educators and authors in the United States.

This sentence would most likely be found in

Ⓔ an autobiography.

Ⓕ a fiction text.

Ⓖ a poem.

Ⓗ a biography.

---

5. Tiger! Tiger! Burning bright
In the forests of the night,

These lines would most likely be found in a

Ⓐ fable.

Ⓑ poem.

Ⓒ myth.

Ⓓ fairy tale.

---

6. Before you begin your bike ride, you should make sure that you are wearing the appropriate protective gear.

This sentence would most likely be found in

Ⓔ nonfiction text.

Ⓕ fiction text.

Ⓖ a biography.

Ⓗ none of the above.

---

7. The hare was once boasting of his speed before the other animals.

This sentence would most likely be found in

Ⓐ fiction text.

Ⓑ a fairy tale.

Ⓒ a myth.

Ⓓ a fable.

---

8. And so the village folk lived happily ever after.

This sentence would most likely be found in

Ⓔ a fable.

Ⓕ a fairy tale.

Ⓖ a folktale.

Ⓗ fiction text.

Fiction

Directions: Read the passage and then fill in the answer circles for your choices.

The Wolf and the Fox

Adapted by the Brothers Grimm

The wolf and the fox lived together in the woods. The wolf made the fox do whatever he wanted and the fox obeyed the wolf because he was weaker. The fox hated the wolf and he longed for the day when he could be rid of him.

One day the wolf said, "Red Fox, get me something to eat or else I will eat you myself!" The fox answered, "I know a farm where there are two young lambs." "Very good," said the wolf. They went to the farm and the fox stole the lamb. He took it to the wolf and then left. The wolf devoured it, but he was not satisfied. He went to get the other lamb, but he made so much noise that the mother of the lamb heard him. She began to cry out so that the farmers came running. They found the wolf and beat him so badly that he went to the fox limping and howling. "You have misled me finely," said he. "I went to get the other lamb and the farmers surprised me and have beaten me to a jelly." The fox replied, "Why are you such a glutton?"

The next day they went into the country. The greedy wolf said, "Red Fox, get me something to eat or I will eat you myself!" The fox said, "I know a farmhouse where the wife is baking pancakes." So they went there, and the fox slipped round the house and sniffed about until he discovered the pancakes. He snatched six and carried them to the wolf. "There is something for you to eat," he said and then went his way. The wolf swallowed down the pancakes and said, "They make one want more." He went and tore the whole dish down so that it broke in pieces. This made such a noise that the woman came out, and she called the people, who hurried there. They beat the wolf with sticks. Still with two lame legs, and howling loudly, he returned to the fox in the forest. "How abominably you have misled me," cried he. "The peasants caught me and tanned my skin." But the fox replied, "Why are you such a glutton?"

On the third day, when they were out together, and the wolf could only limp along painfully, he again said, "Red Fox, get me something to eat or I will eat you myself!" The fox answered, "I know a man who has been killing, and the salted meat is lying in a barrel in the cellar. The wolf said, "This time I'll go when you do so that you can help me if I am not able to get away." "I am willing," said the fox, and he showed the wolf the way to the cellar. There was meat in abundance. The wolf attacked it instantly and thought there was plenty of time before he needed to leave. The fox liked it also, but he looked around and often ran to the hole by which they had come in, to find out if his body was still thin enough to slip through it. The wolf asked, "Dear Fox, why you are running here and there and jumping in and out?" "I must see that no one is coming," replied the crafty fellow. "Good, Fox," said the wolf, "I shall not leave until the barrel is empty."

In the meantime, the farmer heard the noise of the fox's jumping and came into the cellar. When the fox saw him he was out of the hole at one bound. The wolf tried to follow him, but he was so fat he got stuck. The farmer beat the wolf dead. So the fox bounded into the forest, glad to be rid of the old glutton forever.

Fiction (cont.)

1. Why does the fox do whatever the wolf says?
   - (A) He loves the wolf.
   - (B) He fears the wolf.
   - (C) The wolf is bigger and stronger.
   - (D) The fox is not very bright.

2. Which of the following shows the correct sequence of events?
   - (E) The fox and the wolf eat pancakes, meat, then lambs.
   - (F) The fox and the wolf eat meat, lambs, then pancakes.
   - (G) The fox and the wolf eat lambs, pancakes, then meat.
   - (H) The fox and the wolf eat lambs, chicken, then pancakes.

3. The word *glutton* most likely means someone who is
   - (A) greedy.
   - (B) hungry.
   - (C) mean.
   - (D) sly.

4. How does the man get the salted meat?
   - (E) He buys it at the supermarket.
   - (F) He hunts and kills animals.
   - (G) He steals it from his neighbor.
   - (H) He orders it from the fox.

5. Why does the fox keep running to the hole?
   - (A) He is protecting the wolf.
   - (B) He is making sure that he could still fit through the hole.
   - (C) He is nervous.
   - (D) He needs the exercise.

6. What does the fox tell the wolf about why he is running to the hole?
   - (E) He's checking to make sure no one is coming.
   - (F) He's getting fresh air.
   - (G) He's looking for their friends.
   - (H) He's not feeling well.

7. Why can't the wolf escape from the hole?
   - (A) He's too slow.
   - (B) He's too fat.
   - (C) He's afraid.
   - (D) He doesn't want to.

8. Which of the following statements best describes the author's point of view?
   - (E) Don't be mean to others.
   - (F) Don't help others.
   - (G) It's better to be smart than strong.
   - (H) It's better to be a wolf than a fox.

Poetry

Directions: Read the poem and the fill in the answer circles for your choices.

Block City

By

Robert Louis Stevenson

① What are you able to build with your blocks?

② Castles and palaces, temples and docks.

③ Rain may keep raining, and others go roam,

④ But I can be happy and building at home.

⑤ Let the sofa be mountains, the carpet the sea,

⑥ There I'll establish a city for me:

⑦ A kirk and a mill and a palace beside,

⑧ And a harbour as well where my vessels may ride.

⑨ Great is the palace with pillar and wall,

⑩ A sort of a tower on top of it all,

⑪ And steps coming down in an orderly way

⑫ To where my toy vessels lie safe in the bay.

⑬ This one is for sailing and that one is moored:

⑭ Hark to the song of the sailors aboard!

⑮ And see, on the steps of my palace, the kings

⑯ Coming and going with presents and things!

⑰ Yet as I saw it, I see it again,

⑱ The kirk and the palace, the ships and the men,

⑲ And as long as I live and where'er I may be,

⑳ I'll always remember my town by the sea.

1. Lines three and four most likely mean that
   - (A) the child likes to play alone.
   - (B) the child hates to play alone.
   - (C) the child is happy as long as he can build with his blocks.
   - (D) rainy days are very dull.

2. What do the sofa and the carpet become?
   - (E) hills and valleys
   - (F) mountains and seas
   - (G) palaces
   - (H) churches

3. The word *vessels* refers to
   - (A) toy soldiers.
   - (B) toy sailors.
   - (C) toy ships.
   - (D) kings.

4. What do the kings bring?
   - (E) boats
   - (F) money
   - (G) presents
   - (H) None of the above

5. Where is this poem most likely set?
   - (A) indoors
   - (B) outdoors
   - (C) in a classroom
   - (D) None of the above

6. What does the word *moored* in line 13 mean?
   - (E) damaged
   - (F) docked
   - (G) drifting
   - (H) sinking

7. The steps of the palace are described as being
   - (A) orderly.
   - (B) steep.
   - (C) made of wood.
   - (D) old.

8. The theme of this poem is
   - (E) how to keep busy on a rainy day.
   - (F) how to build things with blocks.
   - (G) happiness.
   - (H) the imagination of children.

9. In the first stanza of the poem which lines rhyme?
   - (A) one and two
   - (B) three and four
   - (C) Both A and B
   - (D) None of the above

10. In the fourth stanza, which word rhymes with <u>moored</u>?
    - (E) kings
    - (F) aboard
    - (G) things
    - (H) None of the above

Fiction

Directions: Read the passage and then fill in the answer circles for your choices.

An Excerpt from *Black Beauty*
by Anna Sewell (published 1877)

The first place that I can remember well was a large pleasant meadow with a pond of clear water in it. Some shady trees leaned over it, and rushes and water lilies grew at the deep end. Over the hedge on one side we looked into a plowed field, and on the other we looked over a gate at our master's house, which stood by the roadside. At the top of the meadow was a grove of fir trees, and at the bottom a running brook overhung by a steep bank.

While I was young I lived upon my mother's milk, as I could not eat grass. In the daytime I ran by her side, and at night I lay down close by her. When it was hot we used to stand by the pond in the shade of the trees, and when it was cold we had a nice warm shed near the grove. As soon as I was old enough to eat grass my mother used to go out to work in the daytime and come back in the evening.

There were six young colts in the meadow besides me; they were older than I was; some were nearly as large as grown-up horses. I used to run with them, and had great fun; we used to gallop all together round and round the field as hard as we could go. Sometimes we had rather rough play, for they would frequently bite and kick as well as gallop.

One day, when there was a good deal of kicking, my mother whinnied to me to come to her and then she said:

"I wish you to pay attention to what I am going to say to you. The colts who live here are very good colts, but they are cart-horse colts, and of course they have not learned manners. You have been well-bred and well-born; your father has a great name in these parts, and your grandfather won the cup two years at the Newmarket races; your grandmother had the sweetest temper of any horse I ever knew and I think you have never seen me kick or bite. I hope you will grow up gentle and good, and never learn bad ways; do your work with good will, lift your feet up well when your trot, and never bite or kick even in play."

I have never forgotten my mother's advice; I knew she was a wise old horse, and our master thought a great deal of her. Her name was Duchess, but he often called her Pet.

Our master was a good, kind man. He gave us food, good lodging, and kind words; he spoke as kindly to us as he did to his little children. We were all fond of him, and my mother loved him very much. When she saw him at the gate she would neigh with joy and trot up to him.

Fiction *(cont.)*

1. Who is the narrator of this story?
   - Ⓐ a young horse
   - Ⓑ a boy
   - Ⓒ a farmer
   - Ⓓ Duchess

2. Where is the story set?
   - Ⓔ the city
   - Ⓕ a meadow
   - Ⓖ a forest
   - Ⓗ a race track

3. Why does the horse not eat grass?
   - Ⓐ She doesn't like it.
   - Ⓑ It makes her sick.
   - Ⓒ She's too young.
   - Ⓓ There is no grass to eat.

4. The fact that the horses talk is an example of
   - Ⓔ hyperbole.
   - Ⓕ personification.
   - Ⓖ metaphor.
   - Ⓗ idiom.
   - Ⓘ all of the above.

5. Who is Duchess?
   - Ⓐ The person who owns the horses
   - Ⓑ The young horse who is narrating the story
   - Ⓒ The mother of the young horse who is narrating the story
   - Ⓓ The master

6. The young horse will probably grow up to be
   - Ⓔ a cart-horse.
   - Ⓕ a hobby horse.
   - Ⓖ a work horse.
   - Ⓗ a race horse.

7. What advice does Duchess give to the narrator?
   - Ⓐ Never kick or bite.
   - Ⓑ Never run through the meadow.
   - Ⓒ Never eat grass.
   - Ⓓ Always listen to the master.

8. The master is described as being
   - Ⓔ difficult.
   - Ⓕ untrustworthy.
   - Ⓖ old.
   - Ⓗ kind.

9. Why do the cart-horses kick and bite?
   - Ⓐ They are mean-spirited.
   - Ⓑ The have not learned any manners.
   - Ⓒ They are not very intelligent.
   - Ⓓ They are following the master's orders.

10. What is the master's nickname for Duchess?
    - Ⓔ Old Girl
    - Ⓕ Sweetie
    - Ⓖ Pet
    - Ⓗ Whiney

Fiction

Directions: Read the passage and then fill in the answer circles for your choices.

From the Greek Myths of Icarus and Daedalus

Among all those mortals who grew so wise that they learned the secrets of the gods, none was more clever than Daedalus. He once built, for the King of Minos of Crete, a wonderful labyrinth of winding ways so tangled up and twisted around, that once inside, you could never find your way out again without a magic clue. But the king's favor changed with the wind. One day he had his master architect imprisoned in a tower. Daedalus managed to escape from his cell, but it was impossible to leave the island because every ship that came or went was well guarded by order of the king.

Daedalus spent many days watching the seagulls in the air. They were the only creatures that were sure of liberty. He thought of a plan for himself and his young son Icarus, who was captive with him.

Little by little, he gathered feathers great and small and fastened them together with thread and wax. He made two great wings like those of a bird. When they were done, Daedalus fitted them to his own shoulders. After one or two tries, he found that by waving his arms he could sail in the air the way a boat sails on the sea. This is how he learned to fly.

He went to work on a pair of wings for the boy Icarus and taught him carefully how to use them. He told him not to take chances in the air. "Remember," said the father, "never to fly very low or very high. The fogs around the earth will confuse you, and the blaze of the sun will melt your feathers apart if you go too near."

For Icarus, these cautions went in one ear and out the other. Who could remember to be careful when he was to fly for the first time? Are birds careful? Not they! And not an idea remained in the boy's head but the one joy of escape.

The day came with the fair wind that was to set them free. Daedalus put on his wings. He waited to see that all was well with Icarus, because they could not fly hand in hand. Up they rose, the boy after his father. The hateful ground of Crete sank beneath them. The country folk, who caught sight of them when they were high above the treetops, thought it was a vision of the gods—Apollo, perhaps, with Cupid after him.

At first there was a terror in the joy. The openness of the air dazed them. When they looked down they became frightened. But when a great wind filled their wings, and Icarus felt himself flying, he forgot everything in the world but joy. He forgot Crete and the other islands that he had passed over. He could barely see that the winged thing in the distance before him was his father Daedalus. He longed for one great flight to quench the thirst of his captivity. He stretched out his arms to the sky and made towards the heavens.

Warmer and warmer grew the air. His arms seemed to relax. His wings began to droop. He fluttered his young hands but he was falling. Then he realized that the heat of the sun had melted the wax from his wings. The feathers were falling, one by one, like snowflakes, and there was no one to help him!

He fell like a leaf tossed down in the wind, down, down, with one cry that overtook Daedalus far away. When he returned, he looked for the poor boy, but he saw nothing but the bird-like feathers floating on the water. He knew that Icarus was drowned.

The nearest island he named Icaria, in memory of the child. But he, in heavy grief, went to the temple of Apollo in Sicily, and there hung up his wings as an offering. Never again did he attempt to fly.

Fiction (cont.)

1. What is Daedalus' job?
   - Ⓐ teacher
   - Ⓑ architect
   - Ⓒ advisor
   - Ⓓ ship builder

2. A synonym for a labyrinth might be a
   - Ⓔ walled city.
   - Ⓕ playground.
   - Ⓖ maze.
   - Ⓗ castle.

3. The King is best described as
   - Ⓐ unpredictable.
   - Ⓑ kind.
   - Ⓒ ungrateful.
   - Ⓓ intelligent.

4. The phrase *in one ear and out the other* means
   - Ⓔ Icarus is deaf.
   - Ⓕ Icarus is sleeping.
   - Ⓖ Icarus is foolish.
   - Ⓗ Icarus doesn't listen.

5. Which of the following shows the correct sequence of events?
   - Ⓐ Daedalus is imprisoned then constructs wings.
   - Ⓑ Daedalus constructs wings then is sent to prison.
   - Ⓒ Daedalus builds a labyrinth for the King while he is imprisoned.
   - Ⓓ Icarus learns to fly then his father is imprisoned.

6. Flying is compared to
   - Ⓔ running fast.
   - Ⓕ sailing.
   - Ⓖ soaring.
   - Ⓗ dancing.

7. How does Icarus feel when he first flies?
   - Ⓐ joyful
   - Ⓑ terrified
   - Ⓒ angry
   - Ⓓ free

8. Which of the following is the best description of the plot of the story?
   - Ⓔ A father gives good advice to his son.
   - Ⓕ A son never listens to his father.
   - Ⓖ A father and son escape from prison, but the son dies in the process.
   - Ⓗ A clever architect builds a great labyrinth for a king.

9. Why couldn't Icarus and Daedalus fly hand in hand?
   - Ⓐ It would arouse suspicion.
   - Ⓑ They really didn't get along that well.
   - Ⓒ It would have been against local custom.
   - Ⓓ They needed both of their arms to fly.

10. What does Daedalus do in memory of Icarus?
   - Ⓔ He burns his wings.
   - Ⓕ He goes to the temple of Apollo.
   - Ⓖ He names an island Icaria.
   - Ⓗ He never flies again.

Main Idea

Directions: Read the paragraphs and fill in the answer circles for your choices.

> Tarantulas are the world's largest spiders. They inhabit North and South America, Europe, Asia, Africa, and Australia. Tarantulas have strong jaws and two venomous fangs. They also have two claws located at the ends of eight hairy legs. These arachnids are carnivorous. They eat insects like grasshoppers and beetles. Some types of tarantulas can live as long as thirty years.

1. The main idea of this paragraph is that

   Ⓐ tarantulas have eight hairy legs.
   Ⓑ tarantulas eat grasshoppers.
   Ⓒ tarantulas are the world's largest spiders.
   Ⓓ tarantulas live a long life.

2. The word *carnivorous* means that tarantulas are

   Ⓔ meat eaters.
   Ⓕ plant eaters.
   Ⓖ both meat and plant eaters.
   Ⓗ cannibals.

> Many of the world's leading scientists believe that our planet is experiencing the effects of global warming. Global warming means that the average temperature of the earth is rising. A small rise in temperature can have a great impact on the planet. It can cause climatic changes. These changes affect plants, animals, and people. Global warming is caused by certain gases, like carbon dioxide. These gases are released into the earth's atmosphere. Most of these gases come from burning fossil fuels. If we don't stop burning fossil fuels altogether, the planet will become uninhabitable.

3. This paragraph explains

   Ⓐ that all scientists agree on the impact of global warming.
   Ⓑ that global warming means an increase in the earth's temperature.
   Ⓒ that global warming has no impact on the planet.
   Ⓓ that many scientists believe that global warming is affecting the earth.
   Ⓔ both B and D.

Main Idea *(cont.)*

4. Which of the following statements is an *opinion*?

    Ⓕ Most of the gases come from burning fossil fuels.

    Ⓖ If we don't stop burning fossil fuels altogether, the planet will become uninhabitable.

    Ⓗ Global warming means that the average temperature of the earth is increasing.

    Ⓘ All of the above

Kwanzaa is a holiday celebrated by many African Americans between December 26th and January 1st. The celebration of Kwanzaa embodies seven basic principles, or values: Umoja, or Unity; Kujichagulia, or Self- Determination; Ujima, or Work and Responsibility; Ujamaa, or Cooperative Economics; Nia, or Purpose; Kuumba, or Creativity; and Imani, or Faith. Kwanzaa is a time when families join together to celebrate their heritage and to give gifts.

5. If the main idea is that Kwanzaa is an African-American holiday, then which of the following would be a supporting detail?

    Ⓐ Imani means faith.

    Ⓑ Kwanzaa is a time when families join together to celebrate their heritage and give gifts.

    Ⓒ The celebration of Kwanzaa embodies seven basic principles.

    Ⓓ Nia means purpose.

---

6. From reading this paragraph, you can deduce that words like *Umoja*, *Nia*, and *Kuumba* are

    Ⓔ French.

    Ⓕ English.

    Ⓖ German.

    Ⓗ Swahili.

STOP

Nonfiction

Directions: Read the passage and then fill in the answer circles for your choices.

The hippopotamus is an animal that lives both in water and on the land. It is native to tropical Africa where it lives in swamps, rivers, and marshes. Its name means *river horse*, but it is not related to the horse. It is related to the hog.

There are two kinds of hippopotamuses living today: the common hippopotamus and the pygmy hippopotamus. The pygmy variety is the less interesting of the two. It is much smaller than the common hippopotamus. It grows to be about two and a half feet high and about six feet long. It weighs between 400 and 600 pounds. It spends almost all of its time in the water because its skin cracks when it gets dry.

The common hippopotamus is a huge, thick-skinned animal. It can weigh as much as 8,000 pounds. Its body is shaped like a barrel, and its legs are short and thick. It usually stands a little less than five feet high and may be as long as 14 feet, including its tail. Its feet rest flat on the ground and have four toes each. Its head is large and lumpy and so heavy that the animal usually leans its chin on something for support when it comes out of the water. Its eyes and ears are small and pig-like. Its nostrils are set high on its head so that it can raise its head to breathe and still stay safely beneath the water.

The hippopotamus has a really enormous mouth that can spread open three or four feet. It has powerful teeth and strong tusks which can grow to a length of four feet or more. With these tusks and teeth, the hippopotamus can easily root up and chew the toughest grass and stems. A full-grown hippopotamus has a stomach over ten feet long that can hold five to six bushels of grass. A bushel is equal to eight gallons.

1. This passage is mainly about
   - Ⓐ the common hippopotamus.
   - Ⓑ the pygmy hippopotamus.
   - Ⓒ tropical Africa.
   - Ⓓ pig-like animals.

2. The word *native* means
   - Ⓔ related to.
   - Ⓕ originating in a place.
   - Ⓖ unusual.
   - Ⓗ plentiful.

3. Which of the following is an opinion?
   - Ⓐ The pygmy variety is the less interesting of the two.
   - Ⓑ The common hippopotamus is a huge, thick-skinned animal.
   - Ⓒ A bushel is equal to eight gallons.
   - Ⓓ Its feet rest flat on the ground and have four toes each.

4. The word *hipppopotamus* means
   - Ⓔ related to the hog.
   - Ⓕ large and lumpy.
   - Ⓖ tropical animal.
   - Ⓗ river horse.

5. The body of the common hippopotamus is shaped like

Ⓐ a trunk.

Ⓑ a barrel.

Ⓒ a pig.

Ⓓ a horse.

6. Why does the common hippopotamus like to rest its head on something?

Ⓔ Because it's very heavy.

Ⓕ Because it's a lazy animal.

Ⓖ To release the water from its nostrils.

Ⓗ To help it digest its food.

7. You can infer from the information given that the hippopotamus is

Ⓐ a carnivore.

Ⓑ an omnivore.

Ⓒ a herbivore.

Ⓓ an eater of fish.

8. The tusks of the common hippopotamus help it

Ⓔ to fight its enemies.

Ⓕ to attract a mate.

Ⓖ to dig up grass and stems.

Ⓗ to build a shelter.

9. Which of the following statements is true?

Ⓐ A full-grown hippopotamus has a stomach over ten feet long.

Ⓑ The pygmy variety is the less interesting of the two.

Ⓒ The common hippopotamus weighs between 400 and 600 pounds.

Ⓓ The pygmy hippopotamus stands about five feet high.

10. The pygmy hippopotamus spends most of its time in the water because

Ⓔ it loves to swim.

Ⓕ it is hiding from predators.

Ⓖ its skin cracks when it gets dry.

Ⓗ it can breath under water.

STOP

Nonfiction

Directions: Read the passage and then fill in the answer circles for your choices.

Florida has several nicknames. It is called the Peninsula State because it is surrounded by water on three sides and juts out into the sea for more than 400 hundred miles. It is also called the Everglades State. The Everglades are marshy grasslands that lie near the end of the Florida peninsula. Sometimes Florida is called the Sunshine State because the sun shines an average of 220 days a year. Florida is warm and sunny in the winter months when much of the rest of the country is very cold.

Because of its mild climate, Florida has become popular as a vacation spot. Tourism is one of Florida's biggest industries. The beach resorts have been famous for many years. Now, in addition to these areas, the inland region around the city of Orlando is the home of Disney World and Universal Studios. These places attract millions of visitors from all over the world. There are also other unusual attractions. Cypress Gardens is the place to go for waterskiing exhibitions, and the Daytona 500 is a 500-mile car race which takes place at the Daytona International Speedway.

In addition to these major tourist attractions, there are national parks, forests, and monuments in Florida as well as many state parks, zoos, and gardens. Florida is a great place to take a vacation!

1. Florida's nicknames is
   Ⓐ the Sunshine State.
   Ⓑ the Peninsula State.
   Ⓒ the Everglades State.
   Ⓓ all of the above.

2. The sun shines in Florida an average of
   Ⓔ 365 days per year.
   Ⓕ 200 days per year.
   Ⓖ 220 days per year.
   Ⓗ 500 days per year.

3. The inland region refers to
   Ⓐ the area on the coast.
   Ⓑ the area away from the coast.
   Ⓒ the land that surrounds a large city.
   Ⓓ Disney World.

4. Which of the following statements is a fact?
   Ⓔ The Everglades are marshy grasslands that lie near the end of the Florida peninsula.
   Ⓕ Florida is a great place to take a vacation!
   Ⓖ Florida is warm and sunny in the winter months when much of the rest of the country is very cold.
   Ⓗ E and G

5. A peninsula is
   Ⓐ a piece of land nearly surrounded by water that juts out into the sea.
   Ⓑ another name for a state.
   Ⓒ Florida's inland region.
   Ⓓ another word for an isthmus.

6. One of Florida's biggest industries is
   Ⓔ winter sports.
   Ⓕ race car driving.
   Ⓖ gardening.
   Ⓗ tourism.

Fiction

Directions: Read the passage and then fill in the answer circles for your choices.

How the Sons Filled the Hut: A Russian Tale

In a small village there was once a father who had three sons. Two were thought to be clever fellows, but the third was so simple everyone said the lad was a fool. One day, the father decided to build a hut at the edge of his pasture. When the small house was finished, he called his sons together and said, "I will give this hut to the one who can fill it completely. Not even a corner is to be left empty."

The oldest son said, "I know the very thing that will do it." And he went off to buy a horse. When he brought the animal into the new hut, the horse filled only one corner of the place.

At once the second son hurried off, saying, "I know the very thing that will fill this hut." He returned with a load of hay, which he hauled into the new hut. The hay filled only half of the little house.

The youngest son scratched the top of his head with one hand. "I suppose it's my turn to try my luck," he said slowly, and then he trudged off to the village. There he wandered about for the rest of the day. Toward the evening, as the lights began to shine from the cottage windows, the young lad suddenly slapped his thigh and laughed out loud. "Now I know the very thing that will do it!" he exclaimed.

Like a flash, he bought a fat candle and hurried to the new hut. Once inside, the lad lit the candle, and the whole hut was filled with light, including every corner, nook, and cranny. And so the simple son, whom everyone thought was a fool, won the new little house for himself.

1. This tale is an example of
   (A) an adventure story.
   (B) a fable.
   (C) an autobiography.
   (D) a mystery.

2. Which paragraph describes what the second son brought to fill the hut?
   (E) 1
   (F) 4
   (G) 3
   (H) 5

3. Why did the oldest son put a horse in the hut?
   (A) A horse was the biggest thing he could find.
   (B) He wanted his younger brother to inherit the hut.
   (C) He thought the horse would fill the hut.
   (D) He wasn't as clever as his two brothers.

4. In paragraph 5, *Like a flash* is an example of
   (E) a simile.
   (F) a sentence.
   (G) a metaphor.
   (H) an idiom.

5. By the end of the story, the villagers were probably
   (A) tired.
   (B) surprised.
   (C) angry.
   (D) confused.

6. The theme of this story is
   (E) that people can be smarter than you think they are.
   (F) the relationship between fathers and sons.
   (G) that candles fill up rooms with light.
   (H) that younger brothers can be smarter.

STOP

Nonfiction

Directions: Read the instructions and then fill in the answer circles for your choices on the following page.

Assembling Your Redwood Birdhouse

Kit Includes

2 roof pieces 4" by 6"

2 side pieces 3 ½" x 4 ½"

1 front piece 3 ½" x 4" with pointed top and two holes

1 end piece 3 ½" by 4" pointed top

1 floor piece 4" x 4 ½"

1 round perch 2 ½" long

1 wire hanger with two ¼" wood screws

If you find any of these parts to your birdhouse missing, write or email for replacements.

Bird Lover's Club

**2314 W. Aviary Drive
Preston, MN 31579-4007
www.birdlover.com**

Assembly

1. Place the floor piece flat and glue the two side pieces to it at a 90 degree angle.

2. Glue the front and end pieces to the three pieces.

3. Glue the two roof pieces in place and let sit overnight or until the glue is dry.

4. Push the round perch into the small hole on the front of the birdhouse.

5. Fasten with wire hanger to the roof by putting the wood screws in the two predrilled holes.

6. Find a secluded spot in a tree or under the eaves of your roof to hang your birdhouse. Soon you will have a family of happy birds nesting there.

7. Use a pair of binoculars to watch the happy family of birds that will be nesting there.

GO

Nonfiction *(cont.)*

1. *Assembling* in the title means
   - (A) putting together.
   - (B) gluing wood.
   - (C) hanging.
   - (D) bird watching.

2. How is the birdhouse fastened to the roof?
   - (E) by a 90 degree angle.
   - (F) by a wire hanger.
   - (G) by wood screws.
   - (H) by the perch.

3. Why do the instructions say "let sit overnight" in step 3?
   - (A) so you won't scare the birds away.
   - (B) to see if it will fall apart.
   - (C) because it's time to go to bed.
   - (D) to let the glue dry.

4. In step 5, what are *predrilled* holes?
   - (E) Holes for the birds to enter.
   - (F) Holes for the perch.
   - (G) Holes that have already been drilled.
   - (H) Holes to let the air in.

5. You would probably find these assembly instructions in
   - (A) a magazine on birds.
   - (B) an encyclopedia.
   - (C) the newspaper.
   - (D) a news bulletin.

6. Why do you think that step 7 is included in the instructions?
   - (E) to make sure you have binoculars
   - (F) so you could watch the birds without disturbing them
   - (G) to tell you to attract happy birds
   - (H) to give you the bird club address and email

Fiction

Directions: Read the passage and then fill in the answer circles for your choices on the following page.

The Best Baker

Mrs. Swenson and Mr. Olson each put signs in the windows of their bakeries saying, "The Best Baker in the Land". Back and forth they argued, saying, "I am the best", "No, I am the best". The townspeople soon wearied of their constant bickering.

One day, the mayor announced that the King was coming to look for a new royal baker. "If one of you wins," he told them, "it will be a great honor."

The two bakers baked for days to impress the King. When he arrived, he looked over the cakes, cookies, and pies and cried, "But where is the bread?" The two bakers looked at each other and said, "Bread?"

"You must bake bread for the King!" cried the Mayor.

"I only have a little flour and milk left," said Mrs. Swenson.

"I only have a little yeast and butter," said Mr. Olson.

"Fine," said the King, "then together you can bake bread."

Mr. Olson took his yeast and butter over to Mrs. Swenson's bakery. Mrs. Swenson put on her apron. Mr. Olson put on his hat. The bread was finished when the Mayor ran in. "Hurry! The King is getting impatient." He grabbed the bread from the oven and raced down the street, with Mrs. Swenson and Mr. Olson behind him.

The King tasted the bread and smiled. "This is the best bread I have ever tasted! You will both be royal bakers and bake my bread together."

GO

Fiction *(cont.)*

1. Why were the bakers surprised when the King asked for bread?
   - (A) They didn't know how to bake bread.
   - (B) Kings don't normally eat bread.
   - (C) They thought he wanted fancy pastries.
   - (D) They had already baked bread.

2. What is the setting of this story?
   - (E) a castle
   - (F) a small town
   - (G) a big city
   - (H) a town hall

3. What lesson did the two bakers learn?
   - (A) Baking bread is fun.
   - (B) Working together brings success.
   - (C) Keeping food on your shelves is important.
   - (D) The King is always right.

4. The word *honor* means
   - (E) king.
   - (F) mayor.
   - (G) recognition.
   - (H) tradition.

5. The word *impatient* means
   - (A) restless.
   - (B) angry.
   - (C) tired.
   - (D) bossy.

6. The genre of this story is probably
   - (E) nonfiction.
   - (F) biography.
   - (G) fable.
   - (H) romance.

7. The word *wearied* means
   - (A) worried.
   - (B) fought.
   - (C) tired.
   - (D) baked.

8. What ingredients was Mr. Olson missing to make bread?
   - (E) flour and milk
   - (F) yeast and butter
   - (G) water and eggs
   - (H) flour and butter

Fiction

Directions: Read the passage and then fill in the answer circles for your choices.

A Fable by Aesop

A slave named Androcles escaped from his master and fled to the forest. As he was wandering around he came upon a lion lying down moaning and groaning. At first he turned to run, but finding that the lion did not pursue him, he turned back and went up to him. As he came near, the lion put out his paw, which was all swollen and bleeding. Androcles found that a huge thorn had got into it and was causing all of the pain. He pulled out the thorn and bound up the paw of the lion, who was soon able to rise and lick the hand of Androcles like a dog. Then the lion took Androcles to his cave and every day brought him meat from which to live.

After a time though, Androcles and the lion were captured. The slave was sentenced to be thrown to the lion after the lion had been kept without food for several days. The Emperor and all of his Court came to see the spectacle. Androcles was led out into the middle of the arena. The lion was let loose from his den and he rushed and roared toward his victim. But as soon as the lion came near to Androcles he recognized his friend and licked his hand just like a friendly dog. The Emperor was surprised to see this. He sent for Androcles who told him the whole story. The Emperor was so astonished that he freed Androcles and let the lion return to his forest.

1. Which is the correct sequence of events in the story?
   - Ⓐ Androcles is captured then removes the thorn from the lion's paw.
   - Ⓑ Androcles escapes and then removes the thorn from the lion's paw.
   - Ⓒ Androcles escapes, is sent to the arena, then removes the thorn from the lion's paw.
   - Ⓓ The lion is returned to the forest then Androcles removes the thorn from his paw.

2. How did Androcles know that is was safe to approach the lion in the forest?
   - Ⓔ The lion was sleeping.
   - Ⓕ The lion was on a large leash.
   - Ⓖ He already knew the lion.
   - Ⓗ The lion did not pursue him.

3. How did the lion show gratitude to Androcles immediately after he removed the thorn?
   - Ⓐ He licked his hand.
   - Ⓑ He brought him meat.
   - Ⓒ He did not kill him.
   - Ⓓ He rolled on his back and purred.

4. What was Androcles' punishment for escaping?
   - Ⓔ He was sent to prison.
   - Ⓕ He was to be starved to death.
   - Ⓖ He was to be beaten.
   - Ⓗ He was to be fed to the lion.

5. Why was the lion kept without food for several days?
   - Ⓐ To make him more vicious.
   - Ⓑ To punish him.
   - Ⓒ He wasn't hungry.
   - Ⓓ He was sick.

6. The theme of this fable is
   - Ⓔ kindness.
   - Ⓕ intelligence.
   - Ⓖ gratitude.
   - Ⓗ slavery.

Nonfiction

Directions: Read the passage and then fill in the answer circles for your choices.

In order to better understand the world in which we live, geographers divide the earth up into regions, which are areas on the planet that have common characteristics. For example, a region may have the same type of weather, industry, or landforms.

The United States is divided into four regions: the Northeast, the South, the Midwest, and the West. Each one of these regions has some unique cultural and physical characteristics. Many large metropolitan areas like New York City, Philadelphia, Boston, and Washington, DC are located in the Northeast region. This region of the United States is also very culturally diverse. For many immigrants, the Northeast region is the gateway to the United States.

The Midwest region is known for its open plains, which are good for farming. This region is often called the *breadbasket* of the United States because so much food is grown there. The five Great Lakes are also located in the Midwest.

Texas, Arkansas, and Florida are just some of the states that are located in the South region. Two of our most recent presidents, President George W. Bush and President Bill Clinton are from this region. The South is also famous for Tex-Mex and Cajun food.

The largest region in the United States is the West. This region contains California, Alaska, and Hawaii. The Rocky Mountains are located in the West, as well as the Grand Canyon. There are deserts, beaches, and snow-covered mountains here. Many people vacation in this region every year because of the weather. The West is the most beautiful region in the United States.

1. According to this passage, how many regions are in the United States?
   Ⓐ five
   Ⓑ four
   Ⓒ six
   Ⓓ three

2. Which region was referred to as the gateway to the United States?
   Ⓔ West
   Ⓕ South
   Ⓖ Midwest
   Ⓗ Northeast

GO

3. Why is the Midwest referred to as the *breadbasket*?

   (A) It is a large farming region.

   (B) Midwesterners really like to eat bread.

   (C) It is shaped like a breadbasket.

   (D) Breadbaskets are manufactured there.

4. In what region would you find Lake Superior?

   (E) Northeast

   (F) Midwest

   (G) South

   (H) Michigan

5. A region is

   (A) any area on one of the planets.

   (B) the Midwest area of the United States.

   (C) an area on Earth with common characteristics.

   (D) another name for the planet Earth.

6. Tex-Mex food is probably a combination of food from

   (E) Texas and Mexico.

   (F) Texas and Florida.

   (G) Texas and Cajun.

   (H) Texas and Arkansas.

7. Which of the following statements is an *opinion*?

   (A) The largest region in the United States is the West.

   (B) The five Great Lakes are also located in the Midwest.

   (C) The West is the most beautiful region.

   (D) The United States is divided into four regions.

8. Dividing the earth into regions helps people to

   (E) make travel arrangements.

   (F) understand the world.

   (G) get from place to place.

   (H) decide where they might want to live.

STOP

Nonfiction

Directions: Read the passage and then fill in the answer circles for your choices.

After the bleak, cold days of winter, spring comes at last. We begin to get more hours of sunlight each day. That is when life in and around many ponds starts to come alive.

Ponds are like small lakes of water. Some are left behind after the rivers overflow their banks each spring. When the rivers recede, little ponds of water are left in the surrounding low areas. Some ponds are fed by springs of underground water. It slowly bubbles up through the ground and keeps them fresh and full.

In the spring, ponds become home to new life. Plants begin to push up new sprouts. Some, like the water crowfoot, the yellow flag iris, and the spring lilac are soon in bloom. Their flowers add color to the grassy area around the pond. Soon the warmth of the sun spreads through the water. Animal life begins to stir among the weeds and mud at the bottom of the pond. Frogs, toads, fish, and newts mate and lay millions of eggs. Before long the pond is seething with aquatic creatures. Newborn insects, snails, tadpoles, and tiny fish can be seen swarming through the clear water.

You may want to visit a pond in your area this spring. It is a wonderful way to learn more and collect pond life. If you do, remember to observe the wildlife and county codes when collecting any plants or other pond life. That way the pond will continue to support new life year after year.

1. What happens in and around the pond as we get more hours of sunlight?
   Ⓐ Spring occurs.
   Ⓑ Rivers overflow their banks.
   Ⓒ Life in our ponds comes alive.
   Ⓓ Water bubbles up.

2. The words *rivers recede* mean
   Ⓔ rivers go back down.
   Ⓕ rivers overflow their banks.
   Ⓖ rivers get muddy.
   Ⓗ some rivers rise higher.

3. To learn more about ponds look in
   Ⓐ a dictionary.
   Ⓑ a book on a aquatic life.
   Ⓒ a river.
   Ⓓ a plant book.

4. This passage was written mainly
   Ⓔ to warn us of the dangers of river life.
   Ⓕ to entertain us with a story about ponds.
   Ⓖ to give us information about ponds.
   Ⓗ to give us information about frogs.

5. Which of the following would be a good title for this passage?
   Ⓐ Hidden Life in Ponds
   Ⓑ How to Make Your Own Pond
   Ⓒ Plants that Grow in Ponds
   Ⓓ Our Class Visits a Pond

6. On a pond visit, you are asked to observe wildlife and county codes
   Ⓔ because it is spring.
   Ⓕ so you can find the pond.
   Ⓖ to keep you safe.
   Ⓗ so you don't harm the pond.

Fiction

Directions: Read the passage and then fill in the answer circles for your choices.

Roddy was in the fourth grade. He was the shortest boy in the class. His mother died when he was born. He was so tiny, the doctors were afraid he might not live. His father couldn't keep him, so they tried to find him a home, but no one wanted such a tiny baby. He was moved from one foster home to another. Finally, a man and a woman who had no children adopted him. They didn't care that he was small. They loved him just the way he was. To them, he was ten feet tall.

When Roddy started school, he was smaller than the other children his age. Sometimes they made fun of him, and he was often left out of games. Some mean boys in his school called him names and made fun of how short he was. At times he was a very lonely boy.

One day his new parents decided that what he needed was a pet. They took him to a pet shop to pick it out. Roddy was excited. First he looked at the fish, but you couldn't hold or hug a fish. Next he looked at the birds, but you wouldn't take a bird for a walk or have it sleep in your bed at night. Just then he heard a whimper. It came from a cage in the corner. He peeked inside, and there was the tiniest puppy he had ever seen. "He's the runt of the litter," the shop owner said. "I sold all of the brothers and sisters, but nobody wanted him. If you give the little fellow a home, he's yours free."

That night Roddy's parents peeked in to see if he was asleep. There lay Roddy, and snuggled up next to his cheek was the teeny, tiny puppy. Both had found a home where they were wanted and loved.

1. The doctors were afraid that Roddy might not live because
   - Ⓐ his mother had already died.
   - Ⓑ he didn't have a puppy.
   - Ⓒ he was so little when he was born.
   - Ⓓ his father couldn't take care of him.

2. Which of the following is an example of hyperbole.
   - Ⓔ "he's yours free"
   - Ⓕ "he was ten feet tall"
   - Ⓖ "you can't hold or hug a fish"
   - Ⓗ "take a bird for a walk"

3. *Runt of the litter* means
   - Ⓐ only one in the litter.
   - Ⓑ smallest one in the litter.
   - Ⓒ first one born in the litter.
   - Ⓓ biggest one in the litter.

4. After Roddy got his puppy he probably felt
   - Ⓔ sleepy.
   - Ⓕ joyful.
   - Ⓖ little.
   - Ⓗ anxious.

5. Why did Roddy want a puppy instead of a bird?
   - Ⓐ A puppy could sleep in his bed.
   - Ⓑ A bird makes too much noise.
   - Ⓒ A bird needs too many walks.
   - Ⓓ All puppies are free.

6. Why do you think the shop owner gave the puppy away?
   - Ⓔ It was taking up too much space in the shop.
   - Ⓕ It didn't get along with the other pets.
   - Ⓖ He left sorry for Roddy because he's so little.
   - Ⓗ He had trouble selling the puppy.

Directions: Read each sentence carefully. Fill in the answer circle for any word that is misspelled. If all the words are correct, fill in the answer circle for No mistake.

Samples

A. The <u>sled</u> <u>bounced</u> down the hill to the edge of the **streem**.   No mistake.

    Ⓐ   Ⓑ   **Ⓒ**   Ⓓ

B. The <u>bus</u> <u>stopped</u> in front of the train <u>station</u>.   **No mistake.**

    Ⓔ   Ⓕ   Ⓖ   **Ⓗ**

---

1. Ronald was <u>unabel</u> to attend the <u>picnic</u> due to <u>illness</u>.   No mistake.

    Ⓐ   Ⓑ   Ⓒ   Ⓓ

2. Shameka was <u>surprised</u> when she saw the <u>earings</u> we <u>made</u>.   No mistake.

    Ⓔ   Ⓕ   Ⓖ   Ⓗ

3. Our <u>teacher</u> explained that <u>dolfins</u> are <u>mammals</u>.   No mistake.

    Ⓐ   Ⓑ   Ⓒ   Ⓓ

4. <u>Yesterday</u>, I <u>sliped</u> on my way down to the <u>lunchroom</u>.   No mistake.

    Ⓔ   Ⓕ   Ⓖ   Ⓗ

5. The <u>race</u> to the <u>finish</u> line left me <u>breathless</u>.   No mistake.

    Ⓐ   Ⓑ   Ⓒ   Ⓓ

6. The <u>nob</u> on the <u>radio</u> had been <u>broken</u> for weeks.   No mistake.

    Ⓔ   Ⓕ   Ⓖ   Ⓗ

7. My <u>absolute</u> <u>favorite</u> ice cream is <u>choclate</u>.   No mistake.

    Ⓐ   Ⓑ   Ⓒ   Ⓓ

8. My <u>brothers'</u> <u>bicycle</u> was in the <u>driveway</u>.   No mistake.

    Ⓔ   Ⓕ   Ⓖ   Ⓗ

9. If we don't <u>practice</u> we will <u>loose</u> by at <u>least</u> ten points.   No mistake.

    Ⓐ   Ⓑ   Ⓒ   Ⓓ

10. My <u>freind</u> had a <u>bruise</u> when she came out of the <u>hospital</u>.   No mistake.

    Ⓔ   Ⓕ   Ⓖ   Ⓗ **STOP**

Directions: Look for the usage mistake in each item. Fill in the answer circle for the line with the mistake. If there is no mistake, fill in the answer circle for "No mistake."

Samples

A. Ⓐ   Tim went to the corner
   Ⓑ   to wait for the bus. He waves
   Ⓒ   as it approached.
   Ⓓ   No mistake

A. Ⓔ   The river runs south for
   Ⓕ   hundreds of miles before
   Ⓖ   reaching the sea.
   Ⓗ   No mistake

---

1. Ⓐ   I is going to a
   Ⓑ   football game with
   Ⓒ   my family this Sunday
   Ⓓ   No mistake

6. Ⓔ   Him and me went
   Ⓕ   to get a soda after
   Ⓖ   the movie.
   Ⓗ   No mistake

2. Ⓔ   She wouldn't give us
   Ⓕ   no pencil because she
   Ⓖ   told us to bring one with us.
   Ⓗ   No mistake

7. Ⓐ   She weren't doing all
   Ⓑ   of her homework so
   Ⓒ   she got a detention.
   Ⓓ   No mistake

3. Ⓐ   Jamie brung most of
   Ⓑ   the supplies except
   Ⓒ   for the glue.
   Ⓓ   No mistake

8. Ⓔ   My brother, Jose is
   Ⓕ   the fastest runner
   Ⓖ   in the entire school.
   Ⓗ   No mistake

4. Ⓔ   My mother told me that
   Ⓕ   if I behaved she would
   Ⓖ   buy me a candy bar.
   Ⓗ   No mistake

9. Ⓐ   He don't know nothing
   Ⓑ   about what really
   Ⓒ   happened in the yard.
   Ⓓ   No mistake

5. Ⓐ   My sister always
   Ⓑ   ask me a lot of
   Ⓒ   questions about math.
   Ⓓ   No mistake

10. Ⓔ   She get really annoying
   Ⓕ   when she starts to
   Ⓖ   brag about her score.
   Ⓗ   No mistake

STOP

Capitalization

Directions: Read each sentence. Chose the correct way in which to capitalize the word or group of words that go in the blank. Fill in the answer circles for your choices.

Samples

A My favorite book is _____.

Ⓐ *The Call of the Wild*
Ⓑ *The Call Of The Wild*
Ⓒ *The call of the wild*
Ⓓ *The Call Of the Wild*

B My teacher's name is _____.

Ⓔ ms. jane smith
Ⓕ **Ms. Jane Smith**
Ⓖ Ms. jane Smith
Ⓗ Ms. Jane smith

---

1. My favorite holiday is _____.

Ⓐ Fourth of July
Ⓑ fourth of July
Ⓒ Fourth of july
Ⓓ Fourth Of July

2. Mardi Gras is located in _____.

Ⓔ new Orleans, Louisiana
Ⓕ new Orleans, Louisiana
Ⓖ New Orleans, louisiana
Ⓗ New Orleans, Louisiana

3. The _____ is located in Philadelphia.

Ⓐ franklin institute
Ⓑ Franklin Institute
Ⓒ Franklin institute
Ⓓ franklin Institute

4. We honor _____ in January.

Ⓔ Martin luther King, Jr.
Ⓕ martin luther king, jr.
Ⓖ Martin Luther King, Jr.
Ⓗ Martin Luther King, jr.

5. The _____ are my favorite team!

Ⓐ Detroit pistons
Ⓑ Detroit pistons
Ⓒ detroit pistons
Ⓓ Detroit Pistons

6. My mom works for _____ .

Ⓔ Acme Plastics
Ⓕ Acme plastics
Ⓖ acme plastics
Ⓗ acme Plastics

7. The poem is entitled _____ .

Ⓐ "the Road Not Taken"
Ⓑ "the Road not Taken"
Ⓒ "The Road Not Taken"
Ⓓ "the road not taken"

8. *The Wizard of Oz* was written by _____.

Ⓔ l. Frank Baum
Ⓕ L. frank Baum
Ⓖ L. Frank Baum
Ⓗ L. Frank baum

STOP

Writing Punctuation

Directions: Read each sentence and check the punctuation. Fill in the answer circle for the punctuation that needs to be added. If no other punctuation markes are needed, fill in the answer circle for *none*

Samples

A. I put my books lunch, and calculator in my backpack.

Ⓐ .   Ⓑ :   Ⓒ ,   Ⓓ ;   Ⓔ none

---

1. "Hey Harry," Mike called from the window. "Well be there in five minutes."

Ⓐ '   Ⓑ :   Ⓒ ?   Ⓓ !   Ⓔ none

---

2. The attack on the World Trade Center happened on September 11 2001.

Ⓕ !   Ⓖ :   Ⓗ ,   Ⓘ "   Ⓙ none

---

3. The cat pushed its toy underneath the couch.

Ⓐ '   Ⓑ ?   Ⓒ !   Ⓓ ;   Ⓔ none

---

4. I cant tell if it's Dave's baseball glove or not.

Ⓕ '   Ⓖ ?   Ⓗ "   Ⓘ !   Ⓙ none

---

5. Mr. Perez said, "You're not going to pass if you don't do your work.

Ⓐ !   Ⓑ "   Ⓒ ;   Ⓓ ?   Ⓔ none

---

6. Do you think she'll be able to hit another home run

Ⓕ !   Ⓖ .   Ⓗ ?   Ⓘ "   Ⓙ none

---

7. Ms. Jones told us that the bus was leaving at 1145.

Ⓐ ,   Ⓑ :   Ⓒ !   Ⓓ ?   Ⓔ none

---

8. My mother told me to bring a sweater.

Ⓕ !   Ⓖ ?   Ⓗ "   Ⓘ ;   Ⓙ none

STOP

Sentences

Directions: Answer the questions that are in bold. Fill in the answer circles for your choices.

1. The sun rises in the east and sets in the west.
   What type of sentence is this?
   - Ⓐ exclamatory
   - Ⓑ imperative
   - Ⓒ declarative
   - Ⓓ interrogative

2. The cat ran down the street after the mouse.
   What is the simple subject of this sentence?
   - Ⓔ the mouse
   - Ⓕ the cat
   - Ⓖ the cat and the mouse
   - Ⓗ the street

3. My baby brother cried for at least three hours!
   What is the simple predicate of this sentence?
   - Ⓐ baby
   - Ⓑ three hours
   - Ⓒ cried
   - Ⓓ My

4. Measles is a contagious disease. Chickenpox is a contagious disease. Many children get these diseases.
   Combine these sentences. Which one sounds best?
   - Ⓔ Children get measles and chickenpox, which are contagious diseases.
   - Ⓕ Measles and chickenpox are contagious diseases that many children get.
   - Ⓖ Contagious diseases, chickenpox, and measles: children can get.
   - Ⓗ Many children get the diseases measles and chicken pox.

5. Can you please clean up your room?
   What type of sentence is this?
   - Ⓐ exclamatory
   - Ⓑ imperative
   - Ⓒ declarative
   - Ⓓ interrogative

ⒼⓄ

6. Stop tapping your pencil.

   What is the simple subject of this sentence?

   Ⓔ them

   Ⓕ she

   Ⓖ you (understood)

   Ⓗ This sentence has no subject.

7. Toni Morrison is a writer. Toni Morrison is African American. She won the Nobel Prize in Literature.

   Combine these sentences. Which one sounds best?

   Ⓐ The African-American writer, Toni Morrison, won the Nobel Prize in literature.

   Ⓑ The Nobel Prize in Literature was won by Toni Morrison, an African-American writer.

   Ⓒ Toni Morrison, who is African-American and a writer, won the Nobel Prize in Literature.

   Ⓓ Toni Morrison, writer and African-American, won the Nobel Prize in Literature.

8. Karen and her mother went to the mall to purchase supplies for school.

   What is the complete subject of this sentence?

   Ⓔ Karen

   Ⓕ Karen and her mother

   Ⓖ her mother

   Ⓗ the mall

9. The circus clown balanced on a unicycle as he juggled ten plates.

   What is the complete predicate of this sentence?

   Ⓐ balanced

   Ⓑ juggled

   Ⓒ on a unicycle

   Ⓓ balanced on a unicycle as he juggled 10 plates

10. Will you help me organize the inside of my desk?

    What type of sentence is this?

    Ⓔ exclamatory

    Ⓕ imperative

    Ⓖ declarative

    Ⓗ interrogative

Writing Sample

Directions: Read the sentences below and then write a paragraph which directly answers the question.

In many cities and towns in the United States, students are prohibited from bringing cell phones to school with them. One of the reasons schools have banned cell phones is because they feel they distract students from their studies. Do you think this is a fair policy? Tell why or why not.

_____

_____

_____

_____

_____

_____

_____

_____

_____

_____

_____

_____

_____

Research

Directions: Read the questions and then fill in the answer circles for your choices.

1. You are writing a report on former President Rutherford Birchard Hayes. In which volume of the encyclopedia would you look?

   Ⓐ Ru-Sap

   Ⓑ Go-Ja

   Ⓒ Pan-Ro

   Ⓓ The volume needed is not shown.

2. Now you have to look up the location and characteristics of the Sahara Desert in North Africa. In which volume would you look?

   Ⓔ Min-Pam

   Ⓕ Ru-Sap

   Ⓖ Pan-Ro

   Ⓗ The volume needed is not shown.

3. You remember reading something about the War of 1812 in your Social Studies textbook, but you can't remember the page. Where would you look to find the exact page?

   Ⓐ glossary

   Ⓑ table of contents

   Ⓒ appendix

   Ⓓ index

4. Textbooks usually have a mini-dictionary of relevant words contained within in the books. What is this called?

   Ⓔ glossary

   Ⓕ index

   Ⓖ bibliography

   Ⓗ appendix

5. Copying an author's words or ideas and pretending they are your own is called

   Ⓐ stealing.

   Ⓑ literary theft.

   Ⓒ intent to cheat.

   Ⓓ plagiarism.

6. If you were looking for the definition of *finance*, you would expect to find it between which guide words?

   Ⓔ fine–finish line

   Ⓕ filmer–fine

   Ⓖ find–finish

   Ⓗ filbert–film

7. At which of the following web sites would you expect to find information about national parks?

   Ⓐ www.nationalparks.org

   Ⓑ www.parks.com

   Ⓒ www.grandcanyon.gov

   Ⓓ www.vacation.net

GO

The Dewey Decimal System for Nonfiction

(A)	000–099	General Works	Encyclopedias, directories
(B)	100–199	Philosophy	Self-help, psychology
(C)	200–299	Religion	The Bible, mythology, theology
(D)	300-399	Social Science	Politics, education, folklore
(E)	400–499	Language	Languages, dictionaries
(F)	500–599	Science	Mathematics, astronomy, chemistry
(G)	600–699	Useful Arts	Computers, cooking, business, cars
(H)	700–799	Fine Arts	Music, painting, acting, sports
(I)	800–899	Literature	Poetry, plays, essays
(J)	900–999	History	Biography, travel, geography

Using the chart above, choose the categories where you would find the following books.

8. *Favorite Mexican Tales from Folklore* by Guadalupe Ochoa

   Ⓐ   Ⓑ   Ⓒ   Ⓓ   Ⓔ

9. *Chemistry in Medicine Today* by Dr. Alfred Noyes

   Ⓕ   Ⓖ   Ⓗ   Ⓘ   Ⓙ

10. *The Complete Works of William Shakespeare* by William Shakespeare

    Ⓑ   Ⓔ   Ⓕ   Ⓘ   Ⓙ

11. *The Illustrated Bible for Young People* by Morris Baker

    Ⓐ   Ⓑ   Ⓒ   Ⓓ   Ⓔ

12. *Let's Go to Africa!* by Elwaisi Kumaguy

    Ⓕ   Ⓖ   Ⓗ   Ⓘ   Ⓙ

13. *The Encyclopedia of Insects* by Irma Huxley

    Ⓐ   Ⓑ   Ⓕ   Ⓖ   Ⓙ

Standardized Math Tests

While many of the same strategies that students use to navigate other portions of standardized tests apply to math tests, there are a few additional methods with which they should be familiar. Math, after all, is an animal all its own and routinely requires students to solve a plethora of problems by applying a variety of problem-solving strategies.

✓ **Know the Vocabulary!** Make sure you are familiar with all of the related terms that may appear on the test. Area, circumference, and quotient: It would be a shame to get a problem wrong simply because you don't understand what you are being asked to do!

✓ **Underline Key Words!** Read the problem carefully then underline the key words that indicate what you are required to find. Are you looking for the sum? The difference? The perimeter?

✓ **Recognize and Eliminate the Unnecessary!** Often math word problems will provide you with information that you don't need in order to solve the problem. Seek the information you need and ignore the information you don't.

✓ **Select a Strategy!** Often there is more than one way to solve a problem. Chose the strategy which will work best for you. Will you draw a picture? Use a formula? Make a graph?

✓ **Use Estimation and Recognition!** In many cases you will be able to recognize the correct answer immediately. In others, you may be able to simply make an estimate. Estimation and recognition are two strategies that can save you a lot of time on standardized tests.

✓ **Use Mental Math!** Occasionally, you may encounter problems that you can solve in your head. Lucky you! This, too, can save you a lot of time.

✓ **Read All of the Options!** Before you jump to any conclusions, make sure that you read all of the options. Think of the options as helping hands leading you to the correct answer.

✓ **Beware the Lure!** You may frequently encounter traps or lures on math multiple-choice exams. Often one of the options, usually the first or second one, will contain an answer that appears correct but is actually wrong. Have a look:

If you add $11.11 to $32.73, the sum will be

Ⓐ **$43.84 greater than $32.73.** *(lure)*

Ⓑ **$43.84 less than $32.73.** *(lure)*

Ⓒ **$11.11 less than $32.73.** *(incorrect)*

Ⓓ **$43.84.** *(correct)*

This is your average, run-of-the-mill addition problem; however, if you were not careful you might be tricked into selecting either A or B because the first number that you see, $43.84, is actually the sum of $32.73 and $11.11. Of course, neither one of these is the correct answer.

✓ **Use All of the Time!** It's never a good idea to rush through any test, but math tests in particular require that you check and double-check your work. If you have time, go back over as many problems as you can to make sure that your answers are correct.

Number Concepts

Directions: Fill in the answer circles for your choices.

Sample

A. Which of the following is an even number?

- Ⓐ 11
- Ⓑ 8
- **Ⓒ 10**
- Ⓓ 3
- Ⓔ All of these

---

1. Which number is a factor of 24?

- Ⓐ 12
- Ⓑ 6
- Ⓒ 8
- Ⓓ 3
- Ⓔ all of these

2. Which of the following is a prime number?

- Ⓕ 12
- Ⓖ 36
- Ⓗ 12
- Ⓘ 9
- Ⓙ none of these

3. Which of the following is a composite number?

- Ⓐ 3
- Ⓑ 7
- Ⓒ 11
- Ⓓ 28
- Ⓔ none of these

4. What is the value of the digit 7 in 48,<u>7</u>63?

- Ⓕ 7,000
- Ⓖ 70
- Ⓗ 700
- Ⓘ 7
- Ⓙ none of these

5. Which of the following is the largest number?

- Ⓐ 1,754,493
- Ⓑ 1,794,483
- Ⓒ 1,745,493
- Ⓓ 1,950,483
- Ⓔ none of these

6. 50/100 is equivalent to

- Ⓕ .50
- Ⓖ 50%
- Ⓗ $\frac{1}{2}$
- Ⓘ $\frac{3}{6}$
- Ⓙ all of these

GO

Number Concepts *(cont.)*

---

7. Which of the following is the largest fraction?

    Ⓐ $\frac{4}{9}$

    Ⓑ $\frac{7}{12}$

    Ⓒ $\frac{2}{3}$

    Ⓓ $\frac{3}{4}$

    Ⓔ none of these

---

8. What is the value of the digit 9 in 8.09?

    Ⓕ 9 tenths

    Ⓖ 9 tens

    Ⓗ 9 hundredths

    Ⓘ 9 ones

    Ⓙ none of these

---

9. Which of the following is the smallest number?

    Ⓐ .008

    Ⓑ .08

    Ⓒ .8

    Ⓓ 8

    Ⓔ none of these

---

10. 75% is equivalent to

    Ⓕ $\frac{2}{3}$

    Ⓖ $\frac{1}{2}$

    Ⓗ $\frac{3}{4}$

    Ⓘ $\frac{1}{3}$

    Ⓙ none of these

---

11. What is the value of the digit 3 in 9,439,101?

    Ⓐ 30,000

    Ⓑ 3,000

    Ⓒ 300,000

    Ⓓ 3

    Ⓔ none of these

---

12. Which of the following is the smallest fraction?

    Ⓕ $\frac{3}{9}$

    Ⓖ $\frac{7}{9}$

    Ⓗ $\frac{12}{9}$

    Ⓘ $\frac{2}{9}$

    Ⓙ none of these

---

13. Addends are

    Ⓐ the numbers that are added together to get the sum.

    Ⓑ the numbers that are multiplied together to get the product.

    Ⓒ the numbers that are divided to get the quotient.

    Ⓓ another word for numerator.

    Ⓔ none of these

STOP

Computation

Directions: Fill in the answer circles for your choices. Select "none of these" if the correct answer is not present.

Samples

A.

25
x 4

Ⓐ 27
Ⓑ 40
Ⓒ 254
Ⓓ 29
Ⓔ none of these

B.

24 ÷ 8 =

Ⓕ 4
Ⓖ 3
Ⓗ 6
Ⓘ 2
Ⓙ none of these

1.

329
+ 232

Ⓐ 516
Ⓑ 561
Ⓒ 461
Ⓓ 551
Ⓔ none of these

5.

63
x 41

Ⓐ 2,853
Ⓑ 5,283
Ⓒ 3,825
Ⓓ 2,583
Ⓔ none of these

2.

937
45
+ 16

Ⓕ 1,000
Ⓖ 989
Ⓗ 998
Ⓘ 898
Ⓙ none of these

6.

457
x 10

Ⓕ 5,470
Ⓖ 5,570
Ⓗ 4,570
Ⓘ 7,054
Ⓙ none of these

3.

4,329
– 3,779

Ⓐ 550
Ⓑ 560
Ⓒ 505
Ⓓ 551
Ⓔ none of these

7.

600 ÷ 30 =

Ⓐ 2
Ⓑ 200
Ⓒ 2,000
Ⓓ 30
Ⓔ none of these

4.

6,111
– 5,999

Ⓕ 100
Ⓖ 990
Ⓗ 3
Ⓘ 112
Ⓙ none of these

8.

270 ÷ 9 =

Ⓕ 30
Ⓖ 3
Ⓗ 300
Ⓘ 9
Ⓙ none of these

Computation *(cont.)*

9.

7,456	Ⓐ 58,104
x 9	Ⓑ 17,944
	Ⓒ 67,104
	Ⓓ 68,110
	Ⓔ none of these

10.

94	Ⓕ 659
x 7	Ⓖ 658
	Ⓗ 758
	Ⓘ 759
	Ⓙ none of these

11.

67,329	Ⓐ 28,003
− 39,325	Ⓑ 28,000
	Ⓒ 28,932
	Ⓓ 28,002
	Ⓔ none of these

12.

540 ÷ 7 =

Ⓕ 77
Ⓖ 87 R1
Ⓗ 76
Ⓘ 77 R1
Ⓙ none of these

13.

45 ÷ 7 =

Ⓐ 7
Ⓑ 6 R3
Ⓒ 6 R2
Ⓓ 6 R1
Ⓔ none of these

14.

232 ÷ 6 =

Ⓕ 38
Ⓖ 39
Ⓗ 38 R4
Ⓘ 38 R3
Ⓙ none of these

15.

932	Ⓐ 16,844
x 17	Ⓑ 17,944
	Ⓒ 16,944
	Ⓓ 15,844
	Ⓔ none of these

16.

290	Ⓕ 4,050
x 14	Ⓖ 4,150
	Ⓗ 4,600
	Ⓘ 4,040
	Ⓙ none of these

17.

9,324	Ⓐ 494,001
x 53	Ⓑ 494,278
	Ⓒ 495,127
	Ⓓ 494,172
	Ⓔ none of these

18.

68 ÷ 4 =

Ⓕ 16 R9
Ⓖ 16 R5
Ⓗ 17
Ⓘ 17 R2
Ⓙ none of these

19.

532 ÷ 4 =

Ⓐ 130
Ⓑ 131
Ⓒ 132
Ⓓ 133
Ⓔ none of these

20.

29,939	Ⓕ 59,737
+ 29,438	Ⓖ 59,377
	Ⓗ 60,000
	Ⓘ 58,377
	Ⓙ none of these

STOP

Computation and Number Concepts

Directions: Fill in the answer circles for your choices. Select "none of these" if the correct answer is not present.

Sample

A. $\frac{3}{4} + \frac{2}{8} =$

Ⓐ 3   Ⓓ $\frac{1}{2}$

Ⓑ $\frac{8}{12}$ Ⓔ **none of these**

Ⓒ $4\frac{2}{3}$

---

1. Simplify 28/6

Ⓐ $4\frac{1}{2}$ Ⓓ $3\frac{1}{2}$

Ⓑ 4   Ⓔ none of these

Ⓒ $4\frac{2}{3}$

6. $\frac{7}{8} - \frac{5}{8} =$

Ⓕ $\frac{2}{0}$ Ⓗ $\frac{12}{16}$

Ⓖ $\frac{1}{4}$ Ⓘ none of these

Ⓗ $\frac{2}{8}$

---

2. Convert $8\frac{7}{12}$ to an improper fraction.

Ⓕ $\frac{90}{12}$ Ⓘ $\frac{102}{12}$

Ⓖ $\frac{91}{12}$ Ⓙ none of these

Ⓗ $\frac{103}{12}$

7. $\frac{7}{9} - \frac{1}{3} =$

Ⓐ $\frac{4}{9}$ Ⓓ $\frac{6}{12}$

Ⓑ $\frac{4}{6}$ Ⓔ none of these

Ⓒ $\frac{6}{6}$

---

3. Rename $\frac{3}{4}$ to be in its simplest form.

Ⓐ $\frac{3}{4}$ Ⓓ $\frac{4}{8}$

Ⓑ $\frac{1}{2}$ Ⓔ none of these

Ⓒ $\frac{2}{3}$

8. $3\frac{2}{8} + 4\frac{5}{8} =$

Ⓕ $7\frac{7}{8}$ Ⓘ $\frac{1}{2}$

Ⓖ $7\frac{7}{16}$ Ⓙ none of these

Ⓗ $\frac{14}{8}$

---

4. $\frac{7}{10} + \frac{3}{10} + \frac{9}{10} =$

Ⓕ $\frac{19}{10}$ Ⓗ $1\frac{8}{10}$

Ⓖ $\frac{19}{30}$ Ⓘ none of these

Ⓗ $1\frac{9}{10}$

9. $11\frac{5}{6} - 8\frac{1}{6} =$

Ⓐ $3\frac{4}{6}$ Ⓓ $\frac{11}{3}$

Ⓑ $3\frac{2}{3}$ Ⓔ none of these

Ⓒ $\frac{22}{6}$

---

5. $\frac{8}{12} + \frac{13}{12}$

Ⓐ $\frac{29}{24}$ Ⓓ $\frac{15}{24}$

Ⓑ $\frac{21}{36}$ Ⓔ none of these

Ⓒ $\frac{21}{24}$

10. Which fraction is equivalent to $\frac{9}{16}$

Ⓕ $\frac{2}{3}$ Ⓗ $\frac{3}{4}$

Ⓖ $\frac{1}{2}$ Ⓘ none of these

Ⓗ $\frac{18}{32}$

STOP

Problem Solving

Directions: Read each problem. Fill in the answer circles for your choice.

1. There are five different sections in a baseball stadium that holds 10,000 people. Each section can hold the exact same number of people. If the stadium is filled to capacity, how many people can sit in each of the five sections?

   Ⓐ 1,000

   Ⓑ 2,000

   Ⓒ 2,500

   Ⓓ 1,500

2. Orchard Elementary School has 32 classrooms. Each classroom has 32 students and one teacher. If no one is absent, how many people are there in the school altogether?

   Ⓔ 1,024

   Ⓕ 32

   Ⓖ 1,056

   Ⓗ 1,000

3. In order to get to school, Marcia has to walk two blocks east, one block west, and four blocks north. This morning she stopped at the grocery store, which took her two blocks further out of her way. How many blocks did she walk altogether?

   Ⓐ 9

   Ⓑ 10

   Ⓒ 7

   Ⓓ 11

4. Maggie and Mark made 150 cupcakes for the school bake sale. During the first hour they sold 25 cupcakes. During the next two hours they sold 75 more. By the end of the day they only had seven cupcakes left. How many cupcakes did they sell altogether?

   Ⓔ 43

   Ⓕ 100

   Ⓖ 143

   Ⓗ 100

(GO)

Problem Solving *(cont.)*

5. Amanda has five cats. Each cat eats two cans of food per day. How many cans of cat food will Amanda need to buy to have enough to feed her cats for the next 30 days?

    (A) 100

    (B) 50

    (C) 150

    (D) 300

6. Mr. Jones wants to take the 4th and 5th grades classes on a trip to Washington, DC. There are 314 students altogether. Accompanying them on the trip will be 15 chaperones. Each bus can hold 45 people. How many buses will Mr. Jones need to order? Remember, Mr. Jones is going on the trip too!

    (E) 7

    (F) 8

    (G) 9

    (H) 5

7. Jamal's math test grades were 85, 97, 100, 90, 82, and 86. What is his average test grade?

    (A) 95

    (B) 100

    (C) 92

    (D) 90

8. Camilla earns extra money by delivering newspapers. On Monday she earned $22.50; on Tuesday she earned $15.59; on Wednesday she earned $12.75; on Thursday she earned $21.50; and on Friday she earned $23.00. On Saturday she went to the movies and spent $8.00 dollars on a ticket. She bought popcorn for $5.50 and a large apple juice for $3.50. How much money does Camilla have now?

    (E) $95.34

    (F) $17.00

    (G) $78.35

    (H) none of these

Computation and Number Concepts

Directions: Fill in the answer circles for your choices. Select "none of these" if the correct answer is not present.

Sample

A. 24.15 + .32 =

Ⓐ **24.47**
Ⓑ 24.74
Ⓒ 25.74
Ⓓ 25.47
Ⓔ none of these

---

1. .23 + 3.78 + .1 =
   Ⓐ 5.02
   Ⓑ 2.02
   Ⓒ 4.02
   Ⓓ 6.02
   Ⓔ none of these

2. 30.33 + .32 + .08 + .234 =
   Ⓕ 33.07
   Ⓖ 30.964
   Ⓗ 309.64
   Ⓘ 3.0964
   Ⓙ none of these

3. 17.32 – .009 =
   Ⓐ 173.11
   Ⓑ 1.7311
   Ⓒ 1731.1
   Ⓓ 17.311
   Ⓔ none of these

4. 0345 – .247 =
   Ⓕ .0098
   Ⓖ .98
   Ⓗ .098
   Ⓘ 98
   Ⓙ none of these

5. Round 31,279 to the nearest thousand.
   Ⓐ 32,000
   Ⓑ 31,000
   Ⓒ 30,000
   Ⓓ 31,300
   Ⓔ none of these

6. Round 134,478 to the nearest ten.
   Ⓕ 134,400
   Ⓖ 134,470
   Ⓗ 134,480
   Ⓘ 134,490
   Ⓙ none of these

7. Round to the 32.2 to the nearest whole number.
   Ⓐ 33
   Ⓑ 31
   Ⓒ 32
   Ⓓ 30
   Ⓔ none of these

8. Round .790 to the nearest hundredth.
   Ⓕ .800
   Ⓖ .700
   Ⓗ .780
   Ⓘ .790
   Ⓙ none of these

STOP

Computation and Number Concepts *(cont.)*

Directions: Fill in the answer circles for your choices. Select none of these if the correct answer is not present.

Sample

A. Round 199 to the nearest hundred.
- Ⓐ **200**
- Ⓑ 100
- Ⓒ 150
- Ⓓ 50
- Ⓔ none of these

---

1. 367,528 in expanded form is
   - Ⓐ 300,000 + 60,000 + 7,000 + 500 + 20 + 8
   - Ⓑ 30,000 + 60,000 + 7,000 + 500 + 20 + 8
   - Ⓒ 367,000 + 528
   - Ⓓ three hundred sixty-seven thousand five hundred twenty-eight
   - Ⓔ none of these

2. Three hundred two thousand one in standard form is
   - Ⓕ 302,01
   - Ⓖ 30,2001
   - Ⓗ 302,001
   - Ⓘ 302

3. 1,492,799 in word form is
   - Ⓐ one hundred thousand million, four hundred and ninety-nine
   - Ⓑ one million, four hundred ninety-two thousand, seven hundred ninety-nine
   - Ⓒ one billion, four hundred ninety-two million, seven hundred ninety-nine
   - Ⓓ one million, four hundred thousand, seven hundred ninety-nine
   - Ⓔ none of these

4. Which of the following shows the decimals from least to greatest?
   - Ⓕ .502   .40   .53   .45
   - Ⓖ .40   3.45   .502   .5
   - Ⓗ .40   .5   .502   3.45
   - Ⓘ 3.45   .5   .40   502
   - Ⓙ none of these

GO

Computation and Number Concepts *(cont.)*

5. What fraction of the figures at the right are squares?

   (A) $\frac{2}{10}$

   (B) $\frac{5}{10}$

   (C) $\frac{4}{10}$

   (D) $\frac{8}{10}$

   (E) none of these

6. One quarter and two nickels is equal to

   (F) $.40

   (G) $.30

   (H) $.35

   (I) $.25

   (J) none of these

7. Seventeen dollars and twenty-seven cents and fourteen dollars and seven cents is equal to

   (A) $32.34

   (B) $31.35

   (C) $32.33

   (D) $33.00

   (E) none of these

8. To make $21.76 using the fewest bills and coins, you would use

   (F) 2 tens, 1 one, 3 quarters, 1 penny

   (G) 1 twenty, 1 one, 3 quarters, 6 pennies

   (H) 1 twenty, 7 quarters, 6 pennies

   (I) 1 twenty, 1 one, 3 quarters, 1 penny

   (J) none of these

9. In which number does the 9 stand for hundreds?

   (A) 20,893

   (B) 20,941

   (C) 20,409

   (D) 29,620

   (E) none of these

10. Which number is >976?

   (F) 977

   (G) 975

   (H) 952

   (I) 951

   (J) none of these

11. Round the numbers in the problem to the nearest ten to estimate the answer.

   38 + 23 =

   (A) 70

   (B) 50

   (C) 60

   (D) 65

   (E) none of these

12. 0.6 written as a fraction is

   (F) $\frac{6}{10}$

   (G) 6/100

   (H) 6/1000

   (I) $\frac{6}{1}$

   (J) none of thes

Problem Solving

Directions: Read each problem. Fill in the answer circle for your choice. Select "not enough information given" if there is not enough provided to figure out the problem.

1. Rhonda is the tallest. Cheryl is two inches shorter than Rhonda. Monie is one inch taller than Cheryl. Who is the shortest?

   Ⓐ Cheryl

   Ⓑ Monie

   Ⓒ Rhonda

   Ⓓ They are all the same size.

   Ⓔ not enough information given

2. Tiki has $0.83 in his pocket. He has one more dime than he has quarters. What coins does Tiki have?

   Ⓕ 8 dimes and 3 pennies

   Ⓖ 3 quarters, 1 nickel, and 3 pennies

   Ⓗ 2 quarters, 3 dimes, and 3 pennies

   Ⓘ 10 dimes and 3 pennies

   Ⓙ not enough information given

3. The pinball machine costs $0.50 per game. It can take either quarters, dimes, or nickels. How many different combinations of coins can you put into the pinball machine?

   Ⓐ 5

   Ⓑ 7

   Ⓒ 10

   Ⓓ 15

   Ⓔ not enough information given

4. Jim, Jill, John, and Jane each have a book bag. Their book bags are red, green, yellow, and orange. Jane's book bag is green and John's is not red. If Jill's book bag is yellow, what color is Jim's book bag?

   Ⓕ green

   Ⓖ yellow

   Ⓗ orange

   Ⓘ red

   Ⓙ not enough information given

Problem Solving *(cont.)*

5. Jamal, Keesha, Ronald, Maria, and Christopher scored above a 90 on the math test. Their grades were 99, 97, 93, 91, and 98. Jamal got the highest score and Christopher got the lowest. Keesha got a 97 and Maria got a higher grade than Ronald. What grade did Ronald get?

   (A) 93

   (B) 98

   (C) 99

   (D) 91

   (E) not enough information given

6. At the end of a day spent at an amusement park, Lee had $3.57 left. During the course of the day she bought ride tickets totaling $15.75 and a hamburger, salad, and a juice totaling $10.42. She gave the waiter a $1.50 tip. She purchased a book for her sister which cost $7.95 and loaned her brother $3.50 for some cotton candy. How much money did Lee have at the beginning of the day?

   (F) $42.00

   (G) $42.69

   (H) $39.12

   (I) $42.96

   (J) not enough information given

7. Mina is preparing to do a three-hour charity walk. On the first day she walked ten minutes. On the second day she walked 15 minutes. On the third day she walked 20 minutes. And on the fourth day she walked 25 minutes. She doesn't walk on Sundays. How many days will it take Mina to work up to a three-hour walk?

   (A) 30

   (B) 32

   (C) 40

   (D) 33

   (E) not enough information given

8. Ms. Anderson has to be ready for her fourth grade students by 8:45 A.M. It takes her ten minutes to write the morning assignment on the board. It takes her seven minutes to sharpen the pencils. It takes her 12 minutes to distribute the math manipulatives and eight minutes to straighten the desks. At what time does Ms. Anderson have to begin to prepare?

   (F) 8:08

   (G) 8:00

   (H) 8:02

   (I) 7:45

   (J) not enough information given

STOP

Measurement

Directions: Fill in the answer circles for your choices.

Sample

A. What is the perimeter of this rectangle?

Ⓐ 14 feet

Ⓑ 49 feet

Ⓒ **18 feet**

Ⓓ 28 feet

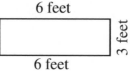

6 feet

6 feet

3 feet

---

1. What is the perimeter of this figure?

Ⓐ 23 feet

Ⓑ 24 feet

Ⓒ 18 feet

Ⓓ 22 feet

10 feet

10 feet

1 foot

2. If each side of a regular hexagon is 4 feet in length, what is its perimeter?

Ⓔ 24 feet

Ⓕ 45,656 feet

Ⓖ 36 feet

Ⓗ 360 feet

3. The width of one side of a square is 2 yards. What is its perimeter?

Ⓐ 4 yards

Ⓑ 16 yards

Ⓒ 10 yards

Ⓓ 8 yards

4. If the perimeter of a rectangle is 48 feet and its length is 20 feet, what is its width?

Ⓔ 4 feet

Ⓕ 8 feet

Ⓖ 24 feet

Ⓗ 10 feet

---

5. What is the area of this figure?

Ⓐ 5 in.

Ⓑ 6 in.

Ⓒ 10 in.

Ⓓ 2 in.

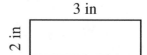

3 in

2 in

6. If the area of a square is 16 feet, what is its length?

Ⓔ 4 feet

Ⓕ 6 feet

Ⓖ 2 feet

Ⓗ 10 feet

7. What is the volume of this figure?

Ⓐ 150 m

Ⓑ 40 m

Ⓒ 17 m

Ⓓ 45 m

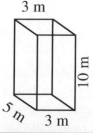

3 m

10 m

5 m

3 m

8. What is the volume of this figure?

Ⓔ 21 feet

Ⓕ 11 feet

Ⓖ 14 feet

Ⓗ 8 feet

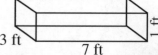

3 ft

7 ft

1 ft

STOP

Measurement and Standard Units

Directions: Fill in the answer circles for your choices.

Sample

A. In four months, Margaret's brother will be one year old. How old is he now?

  Ⓐ 5 months

  Ⓑ 7 months

  Ⓒ 6 months

  Ⓓ 8 months

---

1. How many inches equal one foot?

  Ⓐ 10

  Ⓑ 12

  Ⓒ 13

  Ⓓ 15

2. How many feet equal one yard?

  Ⓔ 4

  Ⓕ 7

  Ⓖ 2

  Ⓗ 3

3. What is the length of this pencil in inches?

  Ⓐ $3\frac{3}{4}$ Ⓒ 4

  Ⓑ 3   Ⓓ $3\frac{1}{2}$

4. Jill just purchased a dozen and a half balloons for the party. How many does she have?

  Ⓔ 20

  Ⓕ 24

  Ⓖ 18

  Ⓗ 6

5. If someone is 720 months old, how many years old are they?

  Ⓐ 55

  Ⓑ 60

  Ⓒ 70

  Ⓓ 35

6. What is the Roman numeral for 29?

  Ⓔ XXXI

  Ⓕ XXXVIV

  Ⓖ XXIX

  Ⓗ XVVIII

7. A recipe calls for two tablespoons of vanilla, but Thomas only has a teaspoon. How many teaspoonfuls of vanilla will he need to equal two tablespoons?

  Ⓐ 6   Ⓒ 2

  Ⓑ 3   Ⓓ 10

8. A quart of milk is half empty. How many cups are left?

  Ⓔ 2 cups

  Ⓕ 4 cups

  Ⓖ 8 cups

  Ⓗ $2\frac{1}{2}$ cups

Measurement and Standard Units *(cont.)*

Ali's Class Roster

Class	Start	Finish
English	8:57	9:43
History	9:45	10:31
Science	10:33	11:17
Math	11:19	12:13
Lunch	12:15	1:02
Library	1:04	1:51
Dismissal at 1:51		

9. How much time is there between each of Ali's classes?

Ⓐ 2 minutes

Ⓑ 1 minute

Ⓒ $1\frac{1}{2}$ minutes

Ⓓ 3 minutes

10. How long is Ali's lunch period?

Ⓔ 45 minutes

Ⓕ 30 minutes

Ⓖ 11 minutes

Ⓗ 47 minutes

11. If Ali arrives one hour late for school, to which class should he go?

Ⓐ English

Ⓑ Science

Ⓒ History

Ⓓ Math

12. If each of Ali's classes, including lunch, were extended 1 and 1/2 minutes, at what time would Ali be dismissed from school?

Ⓔ 1:59

Ⓕ 1:58

Ⓖ 2:00

Ⓗ 2:01

STOP

Measurement and Standard Units *(cont.)*

Directions: Fill in the answer circle for your choice.

Sample

A. About how tall is a regular door?

- Ⓐ 72 inches
- **Ⓑ 7 feet**
- Ⓒ 12 feet
- Ⓓ 12 inches

---

1. How many ounces are in a pound?

   Ⓐ 10　　　　Ⓒ 15

   Ⓑ 16　　　　Ⓓ 12

2. If you wanted to weigh a caterpillar, what customary unit of measure would you use?

   Ⓔ inches　　　Ⓖ ounces

   Ⓕ pints　　　Ⓗ teaspoons

3. If a football field is 100 yards, how many feet is that?

   Ⓐ 100　　　　Ⓒ 150

   Ⓑ 300　　　　Ⓓ 200

4. An adult male elephant can weigh as much as seven tons. How many pounds is that?

   Ⓔ 2,000　　　Ⓖ 10,000

   Ⓕ 1,500　　　Ⓗ 14,000

5. It is about 78 miles from Philadelphia to New York City. About how many feet is that?

   Ⓐ 410,000　　Ⓒ 400,000

   Ⓑ 350,999　　Ⓓ 380,000

6. How many degrees difference are there between thermometer A and B?

   Ⓔ 10°　　　　Ⓖ 0°

   Ⓕ 24°　　　　Ⓗ 50°

7. What is the temperature if it is one degree below zero?

   Ⓐ -1°　　　　Ⓒ -0°

   Ⓑ -10°　　　　Ⓓ Temperatures this low cannot be measured

8. The forecast says that it will be 25° F. What will you be wearing?

   Ⓔ shorts　　　Ⓖ a heavy coat

   Ⓕ sandals　　　Ⓗ a light jacket

9. If the temperature at 8:00 A.M. is 15°, and it warmed up 5° degrees every hour, what is the temperature at 4:00 P.M.?

   Ⓐ 50°　　　　Ⓒ 55°

   Ⓑ 45°　　　　Ⓓ 60°

10. If the combined weight of a litter of puppies is 400 ounces, and each puppy weighs the same, how many puppies are there altogether?

   Ⓔ 5　　　　Ⓖ 9

   Ⓕ 7　　　　Ⓗ 3

STOP

Measurement and Metric Units

Directions: Fill in the answer circles for your choices.

Sample

A There are 2.54 centimeters in an inch. About how many centimeters are there in one foot?

- Ⓐ 72 centimeters
- **Ⓑ 30 centimeters**
- Ⓒ 15 centimeters
- Ⓓ 12 inches

---

1. If an object is 100 millimeters long, how many centimeters is it?
   - Ⓐ 15 cm
   - Ⓑ 20 cm
   - Ⓒ 10 cm
   - Ⓓ 25 cm

2. Which shows the temperatures ordered from least to greatest?
   - Ⓔ 25°C, 32°C, 45°F, 45°C, 60°F
   - Ⓕ 45°F, 60°F, 25°C, 32°C, 45°C
   - Ⓖ 60°F, 45°C, 45°F, 32°C, 25°C
   - Ⓗ 25°C, 32°C, 45°C, 45°F, 60°F

3. Seven liters is equal to how many milliliters?
   - Ⓐ 10,000 ml
   - Ⓑ 1,000 ml
   - Ⓒ 7,000 ml
   - Ⓓ 15,000 ml

4. If you wanted to measure the distance between major cities in California, what unit of measure would you use?
   - Ⓔ meters
   - Ⓕ decimeters
   - Ⓖ centimeters
   - Ⓗ kilometers

5. Ten thousand grams is equal to how many kilograms?
   - Ⓐ 10 kilograms
   - Ⓑ 100 kilograms
   - Ⓒ 1,000 kilograms
   - Ⓓ 100,000 kilograms

6. If a car travels 40 kilometers per hour, how much distance will it cover after 10 hours?
   - Ⓔ 200 kilometers
   - Ⓕ 400 kilometers
   - Ⓖ 800 kilometers
   - Ⓗ 600 kilometers

7. Convert 3000 milliliters to liters.
   - Ⓐ 6 liters
   - Ⓑ 8 liters
   - Ⓒ 2 liters
   - Ⓓ 3 liters

8. How many seconds are there in 20 minutes?
   - Ⓔ 1,800 seconds
   - Ⓕ 1,000 seconds
   - Ⓖ 1,200 seconds
   - Ⓗ 1,500 seconds

STOP

Directions: Fill in the answer circles for your choices.

Sample

A Which figure is a cone?

Ⓐ   Ⓑ 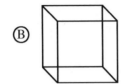   Ⓒ 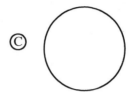   Ⓓ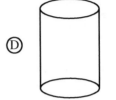

1. What is this solid called?

   Ⓐ triangular prism
   Ⓑ cone
   Ⓒ cube
   Ⓓ rectangular prism

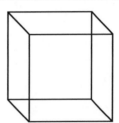

2. What area of this solid is the arrow pointing to?

   Ⓔ vertex
   Ⓕ edge
   Ⓖ line
   Ⓗ face

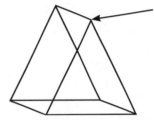

3. What is the darker area of this solid called?

   Ⓐ face
   Ⓑ ray
   Ⓒ edge
   Ⓓ vertex

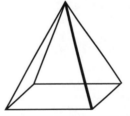

4. What is the darker area of this solid called?

   Ⓔ perimeter
   Ⓕ edge
   Ⓖ face
   Ⓗ corner

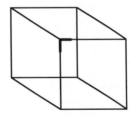

5. How many faces does a rectangular prism have?

   Ⓐ six
   Ⓑ four
   Ⓒ eight
   Ⓓ two

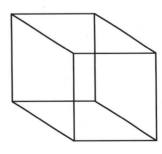

6. A solid has
   - Ⓔ length.
   - Ⓕ width.
   - Ⓖ height.
   - Ⓗ all of these.

7. How may vertices does this solid have?
   - Ⓐ three
   - Ⓑ one
   - Ⓒ four
   - Ⓓ two

8. Which two solids have been combined to create this figure?

   - Ⓔ rectangle and cube

   - Ⓕ cylinder and cone

   - Ⓖ cube and rectangular pyramid

   - Ⓗ rectangular prism and cone

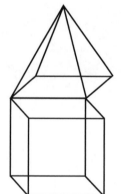

9. Which of these has faces that you can't see?

10. How many vertices does a cube have?
    - Ⓔ six
    - Ⓕ four
    - Ⓖ eight
    - Ⓗ ten

STOP

Geometry

Directions: Fill in the answer circle for your choice.

Sample

A. Which of the following is not a polygon?

Ⓐ Ⓑ Ⓒ Ⓓ

---

1. Which of the following is not a polygon?

Ⓐ Ⓑ Ⓒ Ⓓ

---

2. How many vertices does this polygon have?

Ⓔ three Ⓕ six Ⓖ eight Ⓗ four

---

3. Which of the following does not belong?

Ⓐ square Ⓑ rectangle Ⓒ rhombus Ⓓ hexagon

---

4. How many sides does an octogon have?

Ⓔ four Ⓕ ten Ⓖ eight Ⓗ six

---

5. Which of the following is not a quadrilateral?

Ⓐ scalene triangle Ⓑ parallelogram Ⓒ trapezoid Ⓓ square

---

6. How many vertices does a circle have?

Ⓔ none Ⓕ three Ⓖ four Ⓗ two

---

7. If a polygon has 57 sides, how many vertices does it have?

Ⓐ 50 Ⓑ 57 Ⓒ none Ⓓ 114

---

8. What is another name for a six-sided polygon?

Ⓔ octagon Ⓕ pentagon Ⓖ hexagon Ⓗ congruent

Directions: Fill in the answer circles for your choices.

Sample

A Which of the following is a right angle?

 Ⓐ  Ⓑ  Ⓒ   Ⓓ

---

1. What is this area of the ray called?

   Ⓐ point

   Ⓑ endpoint

   Ⓒ angle

   Ⓓ vertex

4. An obtuse angle is

   Ⓔ greater than a right angle.

   Ⓕ less than a right angle.

   Ⓖ a straight line.

   Ⓗ a square corner.

---

2. In the angle <LMN, which letter represents the vertex?

   Ⓔ L

   Ⓕ M

   Ⓖ N

   Ⓗ LMN

5. Name these lines.

   Ⓐ intersecting

   Ⓑ parallel

   Ⓒ perpendicular

   Ⓓ straight

---

3. What kind of angle is this?

   Ⓐ obtuse

   Ⓑ right

   Ⓒ acute

   Ⓓ straight

6. Of what is this an example?

   Ⓔ line segment

   Ⓕ ray

   Ⓖ point

   Ⓗ vertex

   m   n

7. What is this line segment called?

    Ⓐ JK

    Ⓑ KJ

    Ⓒ both A and B

    Ⓓ neither A nor B

11. Which of these is a ray?

    Ⓐ

    Ⓑ

    Ⓒ

    Ⓓ none of the above

8. What kind of angle is this?

    Ⓔ flat

    Ⓕ long

    Ⓖ straight

    Ⓗ smooth

12. Which of these is a right angle?

    Ⓔ

    Ⓕ

    Ⓖ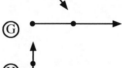

    Ⓗ

9. Describe these lines.

    Ⓐ straight

    Ⓑ intersecting

    Ⓒ perpendicular

    Ⓓ parallel

13. Which of these is an acute angle?

    Ⓐ

    Ⓑ

    Ⓒ

    Ⓓ

10. Which of these is a line segment?

    Ⓔ

    Ⓕ

    Ⓖ

    Ⓗ

14. Which of these is a straight line?

    Ⓔ

    Ⓕ

    Ⓖ

    Ⓗ

Geometry *(cont.)*

Directions: Fill in the answer circles for your choices.

Sample

    A. What is the indicated area of this circle called?

        Ⓐ radius

        Ⓑ **center**

        Ⓒ circumference

        Ⓓ middle

---

1. What is shown on this circle?

    Ⓐ diameter

    Ⓑ circumference

    Ⓒ radius

    Ⓓ area

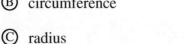

2. What is shown on this circle?

    Ⓔ a chord

    Ⓕ center

    Ⓖ radius

    Ⓗ plane

3. The diameter of a circle is

    Ⓐ 2 times the radius

    Ⓑ 4 times the radius

    Ⓒ 2 times the circumference

    Ⓓ 3 times the center

4. If the diameter of a circle is 15 inches, what is the radius?

    Ⓔ 30 inches

    Ⓕ 7 inches

    Ⓖ $7\frac{1}{2}$ inches

    Ⓗ 2 inches

5. If the radius of a circle is 3.5 centimeters, what is its diameter?

    Ⓐ 2 centimeters

    Ⓑ 10

    Ⓒ 3 centimeters

    Ⓓ 7 centimeters

6. The radius of a circle is

    Ⓔ $\frac{1}{2}$ the diameter

    Ⓕ $\frac{3}{4}$ the diameter

    Ⓖ $\frac{2}{3}$ the diameter

    Ⓗ $\frac{5}{8}$ the diameter

Directions: Fill in the answer circles for your choices.

Sample

A   These two figures are

    Ⓐ   similar

    Ⓑ   alike

    Ⓒ   congruent

    Ⓓ   identical

1. Describe the transformation.

    Ⓐ   flip

    Ⓑ   turn

    Ⓒ   slide

    Ⓓ   bounce

2. Describe the transformation.

    Ⓔ   rotation

    Ⓕ   reflection

    Ⓖ   translation

    Ⓗ   turn

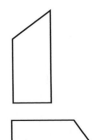

3. How many lines of symmetry does this figure have?

    Ⓐ   two

    Ⓑ   four

    Ⓒ   six

    Ⓓ   none

4. How many lines of symmetry does this figure have?

    Ⓔ   two

    Ⓕ   six

    Ⓖ   eight

    Ⓗ   ten

5. What geometric term describes these figures?

　Ⓐ similar

　Ⓑ cogruent

　Ⓒ not congruent

　Ⓓ very alike

6. What geometric term describes these figures?

　Ⓔ symmetrical

　Ⓕ similar

　Ⓖ opposite

　Ⓗ congruent

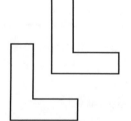

7. Which of the figures has both horizontal and vertical symmetry?

　Ⓐ

　Ⓑ

　Ⓒ

　Ⓓ

8. In geometry, what is a flip?

　Ⓔ A figure that has been moved in a straight direction.

　Ⓕ A figure that has been rotated.

　Ⓖ A figure that has a horizontal line of symmetry

　Ⓗ A figure that gives its mirror image.

Data

Directions: Fill in the answer circles for your choices.

Sample

B To calculate an average you

Ⓐ **add then divide.**   Ⓑ subtract then multiply.   Ⓒ add only.   Ⓓ divide only.

Test Scores #1

James	93
Milton	87
Missy	100
Rhonda	75
Donté	89
Horace	97
Shakira	81

Test Scores #2

James	87
Milton	67
Missy	99
Rhonda	93
Donté	72
Horace	79
Shakira	94

Test Scores #3

James	65
Milton	95
Missy	100
Rhonda	72
Donté	99
Horace	78
Shakira	72

1. What is the class's average score for test #3?
   Ⓐ 83
   Ⓑ 72
   Ⓒ 85
   Ⓓ 35

2. Estimate which student has the overall highest average?
   Ⓔ Donté
   Ⓕ Missy
   Ⓖ Shakira
   Ⓗ Rhonda

3. What is the range in the scores from test #1?
   Ⓐ 25
   Ⓑ 89
   Ⓒ 100
   Ⓓ 75

4. What is the mode score of all three tests?
   Ⓔ 93
   Ⓕ 87
   Ⓖ 72
   Ⓗ 100

5. What is the median score from test #2?
   Ⓐ 67
   Ⓑ 99
   Ⓒ 87
   Ⓓ 79

6. What is Shakira's average rounded to the nearest ten?
   Ⓔ 80
   Ⓕ 90
   Ⓖ 85
   Ⓗ 82

7. What is Donté's test score range?
   Ⓐ 25 points
   Ⓑ 27 points
   Ⓒ 5 points
   Ⓓ 72 points

8. What is Milton's median test score?
   Ⓔ 67
   Ⓕ 95
   Ⓖ 87
   Ⓗ 83

GO

Directions: Carefully examine the data displayed on the following graphs. Fill in the answer circles for your choices.

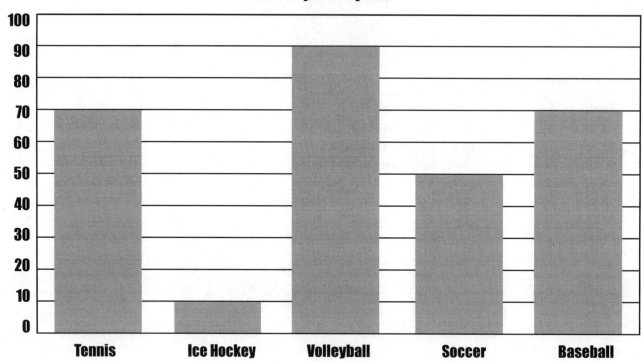

Most Popular Sports

1. Which is the most popular sport?

   Ⓐ tennis

   Ⓑ volleyball

   Ⓒ ice hockey

   Ⓓ soccer

2. Which is the least popular sport?

   Ⓔ ice hockey

   Ⓕ baseball

   Ⓖ tennis

   Ⓗ volleyball

3. How many more students like baseball over soccer?

   Ⓐ 20

   Ⓑ 10

   Ⓒ 35

   Ⓓ 15

4. How many students like both tennis and soccer?

   Ⓔ 150

   Ⓕ 100

   Ⓖ 70

   Ⓗ 120

Data *(cont.)*

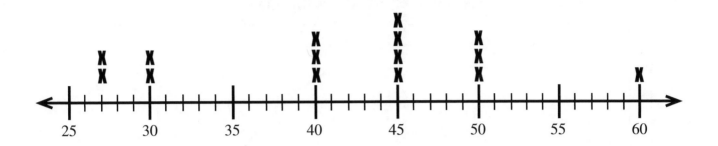

Money in Dollars Earned Weekly by Students

5. How many individual students are represented in this line plot?

Ⓐ 20

Ⓑ 15

Ⓒ 10

Ⓓ 5

6. What amount of money is most commonly earned?

Ⓔ $25.00

Ⓕ $60.00

Ⓖ $45.00

Ⓗ $40.00

7. How many students earned $27.00 per week?

Ⓐ 0

Ⓑ 3

Ⓒ 1

Ⓓ 2

GO

Data *(cont.)*

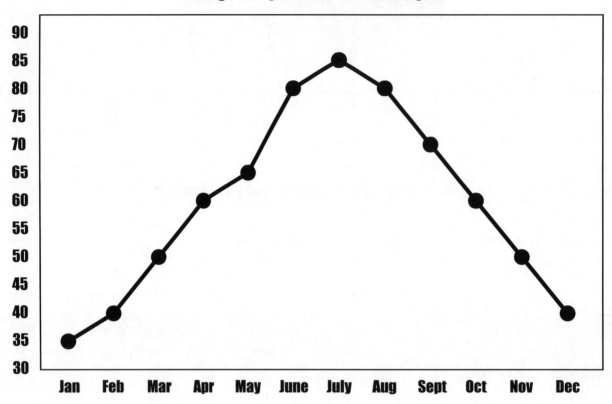

Average Temperature in Philadelphia

8. In what month was the temperature at its peak?

   Ⓔ July

   Ⓕ August

   Ⓖ June

   Ⓗ May

9. In what month is the temperature at its lowest?

   Ⓐ January

   Ⓑ December

   Ⓒ February

   Ⓓ March

10. Between what two months is the smallest decrease in temperature?

   Ⓔ January and February

   Ⓕ June and July

   Ⓖ July and August

   Ⓗ November and December

STOP

Favorite Types of Books

Science Fiction	📖 📖 📖
Biography	📖 📖 📖 📖 📖 📖 📖
Romance	📖 📖 📖 📖 📖 📖 📖 📖 📖
Adventure	📖 📖
Realistic Fiction	📖 📖 📖
Graphic Novels	📖
Fantasy	📖 📖 📖 📖

Each 📖 = 50 people

11. According to this pictograph, how many people prefer adventure novels?

Ⓐ 20
Ⓑ 50
Ⓒ 100
Ⓓ 75

12. According to this pictograph, how may people prefer biographies?

Ⓔ 325
Ⓕ 350
Ⓖ 375
Ⓗ 150

13. If you wanted to show that 75 people preferred horror novels, how many symbols would you need to show on the pictograph?

Ⓐ 2
Ⓑ 1
Ⓒ 3
Ⓓ $1\frac{1}{2}$

GO

Height of 4th Grade Students

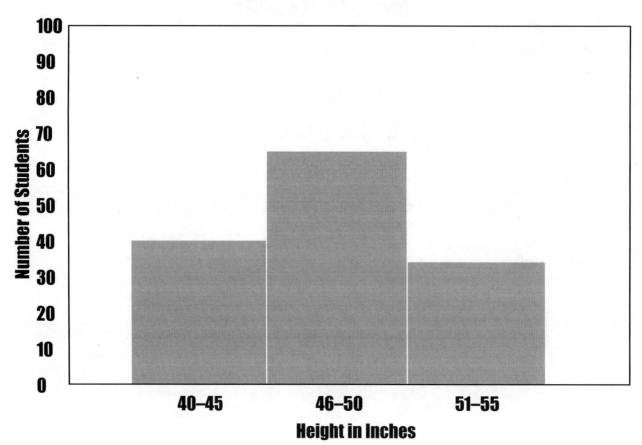

14. About how many students are between 46 to 50 inches tall?

Ⓔ 50

Ⓕ 60

Ⓖ 65

Ⓗ 45

15. This type of graph is called a

Ⓐ bar graph

Ⓑ circle graph

Ⓒ line plot

Ⓓ histogram

16. How many more students are between 46 to 50 inches than 40 to 45 inches tall?

Ⓔ 30

Ⓕ 25

Ⓖ 15

Ⓗ 20

17. How many 4th grade students are there altogether?

Ⓐ 140

Ⓑ 100

Ⓒ 145

Ⓓ 150

Mathematics

Probability

Directions: Fill in the answer circles for your choices.

1. Miguel has a pocketful of change. He has seven quarters, three dimes, and 12 pennies. If Miguel reaches into his pocket, what is the likelihood that he will retrieve a nickel?

Ⓐ certain

Ⓑ likely

Ⓒ impossible

Ⓓ unlikely

2. What is the likelihood that Miguel will retrieve a penny?

Ⓔ impossible

Ⓕ certain

Ⓖ unlikely

Ⓗ likely

3. On the lunch menu today students can have either a tuna salad sandwich or a peanut butter and jelly sandwich. Their beverage choices are juice, water, or milk. How many possible lunch combinations are available to the students?

Ⓐ 4

Ⓑ 6

Ⓒ 2

Ⓓ 12

4. Ms. Anderson brought two dozen pieces of fruit to class with her this morning. Half of the fruits are apples, two are plums, three are peaches, five are bananas, one is a pear, and one is a tangerine. If a student closes his/her eyes and reaches into the box, what is the probability that he/she will retrieve an apple?

Ⓔ $\frac{1}{2}$

Ⓕ $\frac{1}{4}$

Ⓖ $\frac{1}{24}$

Ⓗ $\frac{1}{8}$

5. What is the probability that the student will retrieve a banana?

Ⓐ $\frac{1}{2}$

Ⓑ $\frac{3}{8}$

Ⓒ $\frac{5}{24}$

Ⓓ $\frac{1}{24}$

GO

Probability *(cont.)*

6. The probability of an event occurring is $\frac{3}{4}$. The event is

   Ⓔ impossible

   Ⓕ certain

   Ⓖ likely

   Ⓗ unlikely

7. If you spin this spinner, what is the probability that you will land on a tulip?

   Ⓐ $\frac{2}{8}$

   Ⓑ $\frac{1}{8}$

   Ⓒ $\frac{4}{8}$

   Ⓓ $\frac{3}{8}$

   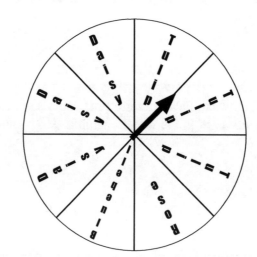

8. How many possible outcomes does this tree diagram show?

   Ⓔ 6

   Ⓕ 12

   Ⓖ 8

   Ⓗ 14

   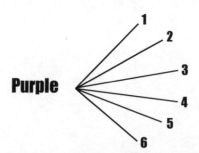

   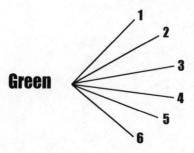

Directions: Fill in the answer circles for your choices.

Sample

A. Which number would come next in this pattern? 3, 6, 9, 12, 15,

  Ⓐ 17   **Ⓑ 18**   Ⓒ 16   Ⓓ 19

---

1. Which number would come next in this pattern? 2, 6, 18, 54, 162

  Ⓐ 450   Ⓑ 400   Ⓒ 490   Ⓓ 486

In	Out
2	14
3	21
4	28
5	35
6	

2. What number will complete this table?

  Ⓔ 36

  Ⓕ 42

  Ⓖ 49

  Ⓗ 54

---

3. What is the rule of the table shown above?

  Ⓐ All numbers were divided by seven.

  Ⓑ Seven was subtracted from all numbers.

  Ⓒ All numbers were multiplied by seven.

  Ⓓ There is no rule. The numbers are random.

---

4. Complete the pattern. □ → ← △ □ →

  Ⓔ

  Ⓕ

  Ⓖ □

  Ⓗ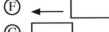

Algebra *(cont.)*

5. There are 537 students in Martin Luther King Jr. School. 140 of them are in 4th grade. How many students are in the other grades?

   Which number expression best translates this problem?

   Ⓐ 537 + 140 = 677

   Ⓑ 537 x 140 = 75,180

   Ⓒ 537 ÷ 140 = 3.83

   Ⓓ 537 − 140 = 397

6. There are 140 students in 4th grade. Each table in the lunchroom can hold ten students. How many tables will be needed to seat the entire 4th grade class?

   Which number expression best translates this problem?

   Ⓔ 140 ÷ 10 = 14

   Ⓕ 140 − 10 = 130

   Ⓖ 140 x 10 = 1400

   Ⓗ 140 + 10 = 150

7. $(17 + 9) - 3 =$

   Ⓐ 26

   Ⓑ 12

   Ⓒ 23

   Ⓓ 29

8. $z + 36 = 723$

   Ⓔ z = 600

   Ⓕ z = 650

   Ⓖ z = 0

   Ⓗ z = 687

9. $(27 - 4) + 13 =$

   Ⓐ 36

   Ⓑ 23

   Ⓒ 17w

   Ⓓ 40

10. $36 - p = 4$

    Ⓔ 32

    Ⓕ 30

    Ⓖ 25

    Ⓗ 41

11. $3 + (9 - 7) =$

    Ⓔ 12

    Ⓕ 10

    Ⓖ 5

    Ⓗ 19

12. Complete the pattern.

  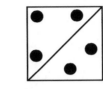

Ⓔ   Ⓕ   Ⓖ   Ⓗ

R	R–11
63	
97	
103	92
11	
42	

13. Which group of numbers accurately completes the table above?
    Ⓐ 53, 86, 0, 31
    Ⓑ 52, 86, 0, 31
    Ⓒ 74, 108, 21, 53
    Ⓓ 51, 86, 0, 31

15. $\dfrac{28}{n} = 7$
    Ⓐ n = 10
    Ⓑ n = 5
    Ⓒ n = r
    Ⓓ n = 4

14. 7 x n = 49
    Ⓔ n = 7
    Ⓕ n = 0
    Ⓖ n = 8
    Ⓗ n = n

16. (7 x 5) – 13 =
    Ⓔ 22
    Ⓕ 35
    Ⓖ 1
    Ⓗ 48

The Water Cycle

Directions: Fill in the answer circles for your choices.

Sample

A. Which of the following does not belong?

Ⓐ precipitation Ⓒ **camouflage**

Ⓑ ground water Ⓓ water table

---

1. Transpiration occurs when
   Ⓐ it rains.
   Ⓑ ground water empties into rivers.
   Ⓒ pores on the leaves of plants give off water vapor.
   Ⓓ there is a flood.

2. When water soaks into the ground and soil, it is called
   Ⓔ a swamp.
   Ⓕ infiltration.
   Ⓖ evaporation
   Ⓗ mutation

3. Ground water flows
   Ⓐ into streams and rivers.
   Ⓑ toward the center of the earth.
   Ⓒ from east to west.
   Ⓓ from north to south.

4. Precipitation can come in the form of
   Ⓔ rain.
   Ⓕ snow.
   Ⓗ sleet.
   Ⓙ All of these

5. If you leave a bowl of water outside, it will continue to decrease in size due to
   Ⓐ evaporation.
   Ⓑ condensation.
   Ⓒ heat.
   Ⓓ energy.

6. How has the earth's current amount of water changed over time?
   Ⓔ There is more water now than there was in the past.
   Ⓕ There is less water now than there was in the past.
   Ⓖ The amount of water on Earth is about the same as it's always been.
   Ⓗ The amount of water on Earth is unknowable.

7. What happens to the water that evaporates?
   Ⓐ It disappears forever.
   Ⓑ It is recycled.
   Ⓒ It flows out into the universe.
   Ⓓ It turns into air.

8. How does pollution in ground water threaten animals and people?
   Ⓔ It smells badly.
   Ⓕ It can contaminate drinking water and irrigation water.
   Ⓖ Plants won't grow near it.
   Ⓗ It is no threat at all.

Earth Science

Directions: Fill in the answer circles for your choices.

Sample

A. A giant wave caused by an earthquake beneath the ocean is called a

- (A) tidal wave.
- (C) ocean current.
- (B) rip tide.
- (D) **tsunami.**

---

1. The crust of the earth is located
   - (A) many thousands of miles beneath the planet's surface.
   - (B) around large mountain ranges.
   - (C) beneath the ocean.
   - (D) just beneath the surface of the planet.

2. Most of the earth's active volcanoes are located in an area called
   - (E) the Ring of Fire.
   - (F) volcano central.
   - (G) the Mariana Trench.
   - (H) Mount Fuji.

3. Magma is
   - (A) a city in Italy.
   - (B) another name for an active volcano.
   - (C) molten rock.
   - (D) the mantle of the planet.

4. A seismograph measures
   - (E) precipitation.
   - (F) ocean currents.
   - (G) continental drift.
   - (H) seismic waves.

5. The largest layer of the earth is called the
   - (A) core
   - (B) crust
   - (C) plates
   - (D) mantle

6. If a volcano is extinct it probably means that
   - (E) it is unlikely that it will erupt again.
   - (F) it could erupt at any time.
   - (G) it needs to be protected.
   - (H) it is no longer of interest to volcanologists.

7. If a building were located at the epicenter of an earthquake, it means that
   - (A) the building will be protected.
   - (B) the building will be in danger of collapsing.
   - (C) the building is located on earthquake proof land.
   - (D) the building is located at a shelter.

8. Metamorphic, igneous, and sedimentary are types of
   - (E) clouds.
   - (F) rocks.
   - (G) volcanoes.
   - (H) oceans.

9. Composite, cinder cone, and shield are types of
   - (A) volcanoes.
   - (B) weather fronts.
   - (C) fossil fuels.
   - (H) rocks.

10. If an animal were caught in a lava flow, what would most likely happen?
    - (E) It would die.
    - (F) It would swim to safety.
    - (G) It would sit down and wait for the lava to pass.
    - (H) It would hunt.

GO

11. A dormant volcano will
    Ⓐ never erupt again.
    Ⓑ possibly erupt again.
    Ⓒ turn into an extinct volcano.
    Ⓓ only eject light lava.

12. In what type of rock would you most likely find a piece of bone?
    Ⓔ igneous
    Ⓕ metamorphic
    Ⓖ shale
    Ⓗ sedimentary

13. The earth's core is comprised of
    Ⓐ lava.
    Ⓑ molten rock.
    Ⓒ liquid metal.
    Ⓓ water.

14. Stalagmites and stalactites are found
    Ⓔ in caves.
    Ⓕ in ground water.
    Ⓖ in vents.
    Ⓗ near fault lines.

15. The Richter scale measures
    Ⓐ the density of rocks.
    Ⓑ volcanoes.
    Ⓒ earthquakes.
    Ⓓ tidal waves.

16. The vent of a volcano is most like
    Ⓔ a door.
    Ⓕ a car.
    Ⓖ a room.
    Ⓗ a trunk.

17. Seismologists and vulcanologists are both
    Ⓐ very smart people.
    Ⓑ areas of scientific study.
    Ⓒ types of scientists.
    Ⓓ types of rocks.

18. Which of the following creates metamorphic rocks?
    Ⓔ pressure
    Ⓕ heat
    Ⓖ chemical change
    Ⓗ all of these

19. Aftershocks are
    Ⓐ small volcanic eruptions that occur after the main eruption.
    Ⓑ a process that creates basalt.
    Ⓒ small earthquakes that can occur after a major quake.
    Ⓓ tension

20. In order to see a stalactite, you would have to look
    Ⓔ up.
    Ⓕ down.
    Ⓖ through a telescope.
    Ⓗ through a microscope.

Space Science

Directions: Fill in the answer circles for your choices.

Sample

A. Sun is to star as Earth is to

  Ⓐ moon   Ⓑ orbit   Ⓒ **planet**   Ⓓ bright

---

1. Moons are best described as

  Ⓐ round.   Ⓑ crater-filled.   Ⓒ natural satellites.   Ⓓ made of cheese.

---

2. The way in which moons and planets revolve is called

  Ⓔ an orbit.   Ⓕ spinning motion.   Ⓖ a projection.   Ⓗ planetary.

---

3. Which best describes the relationship between Earth and the moon?

  Ⓐ Earth revolves around the moon.   Ⓑ The moon revolves around Earth.   Ⓒ The moon is static.   Ⓓ The moon and Earth swap orbits every five years.

---

4. The gravitational pull of the moon is responsible for

  Ⓔ droughts.   Ⓕ floods.   Ⓖ tides.   Ⓗ blizzards.

---

5. Currently the largest planet in our solar system is

  Ⓐ Saturn.   Ⓑ Neptune.   Ⓒ Venus.   Ⓓ Jupiter

---

6. Which best describes the relationship between Earth and the sun?

  Ⓔ Earth revolves around the sun.   Ⓕ The sun revolves around Earth.   Ⓖ The sun does not move at all.   Ⓗ The sun moves from east to west across the sky.

---

7. About how many days does it take Earth to orbit the sun?

  Ⓐ 24   Ⓑ 300   Ⓒ 365   Ⓓ 12

---

8. Mercury, Venus, Earth, and Mars are also called

  Ⓔ orbs.   Ⓕ large rocks.   Ⓖ asteroids.   Ⓗ the inner planets.

---

9. Comets are made up of

  Ⓐ metamorphic rock.   Ⓑ gas.   Ⓒ ice and dust.   Ⓓ clouds.

---

10. Gravity can best be described as

  Ⓔ a natural force between two celestial bodies.   Ⓕ something very serious.   Ⓖ the sticking force.   Ⓗ a type of orbit.

GO

Space Science *(cont.)*

Directions: Fill in the answer circles for your choices.

11. Stars are comprised of

   Ⓐ black holes.   Ⓑ gases that produce nuclear fusion in their cores.   Ⓒ bright stuff.   Ⓓ atoms.

12. Groups of stars that create pictures in the night sky are called

   Ⓔ nebula.   Ⓕ supernova.   Ⓖ constellations.   Ⓗ super giants.

13. What celestial object is about 93 million miles away from Earth?

   Ⓐ moon   Ⓑ Venus   Ⓒ Mars   Ⓓ sun

14. The outermost layer of the sun is called the

   Ⓔ shell.   Ⓕ rays.   Ⓖ corona.   Ⓗ magnitude.

15. When the moon is directly between the sun and Earth it is called a

   Ⓐ lunar eclipse.   Ⓑ sun spot.   Ⓒ solar flare.   Ⓓ solar eclipse.

16. Our sun can also be classified as a

   Ⓔ star.   Ⓕ planet.   Ⓖ moon.   Ⓗ comet.

17. About how many galaxies are there in the universe?

   Ⓐ hundreds   Ⓑ billions   Ⓒ millions   Ⓓ thousands

18. What is your relative location to the Milky Way?

   Ⓔ You are in it right now.   Ⓕ You have never been in it.   Ⓖ You only enter it on leap years.   Ⓗ It is over your head.

19. About how long does it take the moon to orbit Earth?

   Ⓐ 3 days   Ⓑ 24 hours   Ⓒ 365 days   Ⓓ No one knows for sure.

20. Polaris is also known as

   Ⓔ the North Pole.   Ⓕ the South Pole.   Ⓖ the North Star.   Ⓗ Halley's Comet

STOP

Human Body *(cont.)*

Directions: Fill in the answer circles for your choices.

Samples

A. The brain is protected by

Ⓐ intelligence. Ⓑ memory. Ⓒ the immune system. **Ⓓ the skull.**

B. A set of parts that work together is called

Ⓔ in tandem. **Ⓕ a system.** Ⓖ in sync. Ⓗ in concert.

---

1. About how many bones are in the human body?

Ⓐ 550 Ⓑ 206 Ⓒ 1,000 Ⓓ 150

2. The place where two bones meet is called

Ⓔ an axis. Ⓕ cartilage. Ⓖ marrow. Ⓗ a joint.

3. Bones are part of what system?

Ⓐ cardiovascular Ⓑ skeletal Ⓒ immune Ⓓ circulatory

4. Which of the following is an involuntary muscle?

Ⓔ heart Ⓕ triceps Ⓖ biceps Ⓗ hamstrings

5. Red cells, white cells, and platelets can be found in

Ⓐ the brain. Ⓑ the blood. Ⓒ the arms and legs. Ⓓ the lungs.

6. The largest vessels in the body are

Ⓔ arteries. Ⓕ capillaries. Ⓖ veins. Ⓗ aorta.

7. How many chambers does the heart have?

Ⓐ two Ⓑ six Ⓒ one Ⓓ four

8. What surrounds and destroys germs that enter the body?

Ⓔ white blood cells Ⓕ red blood cells Ⓖ plasma Ⓗ vitamins

9. The brain and the spinal chord are part of the

Ⓐ digestive system. Ⓑ immune system. Ⓒ nervous system. Ⓓ endocrine system.

10. The organs in the human body are made out of

Ⓔ tissue. Ⓕ blood. Ⓖ bone. Ⓗ none of these.

STOP

Human Body *(cont.)*

Directions: Fill in the answer circles for your choices.

11. If you wanted to observe cells in the human body you would need

Ⓐ a telescope. Ⓑ a stethoscope. Ⓒ a microscope. Ⓓ a horoscope.

12. Where could you find neurons?

Ⓔ outer space Ⓕ inside the nerves Ⓖ in the muscles Ⓗ in the stomach

13. Ducking when a ball is heading for your face is called

Ⓐ a reflex action. Ⓑ a defensive action. Ⓒ a convex action. Ⓓ smart.

14. The cerebrum is the part of the brain that is involved in

Ⓔ sleeping. Ⓕ eating. Ⓖ thinking. Ⓗ reflexes.

15. The human life cycle includes

Ⓐ childhood. Ⓑ infancy. Ⓒ old age. Ⓓ all of these.

16. If a person is 15 years old they are in

Ⓔ childhood. Ⓕ adulthood. Ⓖ adolescence. Ⓗ infancy.

17. How many senses do people possess?

Ⓐ five Ⓑ four Ⓒ six Ⓓ nine

18. Taste buds are located

Ⓔ on the roof of the mouth. Ⓕ in the back of the throat. Ⓖ on the surface of the teeth. Ⓗ on the tongue.

19. The optic nerve is located

Ⓐ in the ears. Ⓑ in the back of the eye. Ⓒ on the palms of the hands. Ⓓ in the stomach.

20. If you are sick to your stomach you are having a problem with your

Ⓔ respiratory system. Ⓕ digestive system. Ⓖ circulatory system. Ⓗ nervous system.

Energy

Directions: Fill in the answer circles for your choices.

Samples

A Heat is a type of

- (A) force.
- (C) power.
- **(B) energy.**
- (D) resource.

B A thermometer is used to measure

- **(E) heat.**
- (G) precipitation.
- (F) pressure.
- (H) humidity.

---

1. How do the molecules and atoms in a block of ice move?
   - (A) from left to right
   - (C) very slowly
   - (B) very quickly
   - (D) not at all

2. The temperature at which a liquid becomes a gas is called the
   - (E) melting point.
   - (G) tipping point.
   - (F) boiling point.
   - (H) point of no return.

3. When objects get very cold they can
   - (A) contract.
   - (C) crack.
   - (B) expand.
   - (D) shrivel.

4. Heat moving from a hot grill to a hamburger is an example of
   - (E) radiation.
   - (G) convection.
   - (F) conduction.
   - (H) thermalization.

5. The temperature at which a solid turns into a liquid is called the
   - (A) melting point.
   - (C) liquidity point.
   - (B) boiling point.
   - (D) water point.

6. Coal, oil, and gas are examples of
   - (E) fossils.
   - (G) fossil fuels.
   - (F) heat.
   - (H) energy.

7. Trees are an example of what kind of resource?
   - (A) nonrenewable
   - (C) fast burning
   - (B) conservative
   - (D) renewable

8. A nonrenewable resource means
   - (E) once it is used it can never be replaced.
   - (F) once it is used it takes about ten years to replace it.
   - (G) it can be recreated over and over again.
   - (H) it is a non-polluting type of energy.

9. Energy conservation means
   - (A) to try to save energy when possible.
   - (B) to use only solar energy.
   - (C) to use only nonrenewable resources.
   - (D) to plant trees.

10. Which of the following is an example of energy conservation?
    - (E) turning off lights
    - (F) riding a bike instead of driving a car
    - (G) not letting the water run when you brush your teeth.
    - (H) All of these

STOP

Directions: Fill in the answer circle for your choice.

Samples

A. Electricity comes from
- Ⓐ static.
- **Ⓑ charged atoms.**
- Ⓒ convection.
- Ⓓ the air.

B. Who discovered that lightning was electric?
- Ⓔ Thomas Edison
- Ⓕ Thomas Jefferson
- **Ⓖ Benjamin Franklin**
- Ⓗ George Washington Carver

---

1. Receiving a shock from touching a doorknob or brushing your hair is an example of
   - Ⓐ an electrical charge.
   - Ⓑ a current.
   - Ⓒ static electricity.
   - Ⓓ magnetism.

2. Electrical wires are often covered in plastic because
   - Ⓔ plastic is a good conductor.
   - Ⓕ it looks better.
   - Ⓖ it makes it easier to pack.
   - Ⓗ plastic is a good insulator.

3. Which force is responsible for a pencil falling to the floor?
   - Ⓐ gravity
   - Ⓑ friction
   - Ⓒ magnetism
   - Ⓓ erosion

4. Iron nails clinging to a magnet is an example of
   - Ⓔ repulsion.
   - Ⓕ attraction.
   - Ⓖ pressure.
   - Ⓗ inertia.

5. Through which of the following objects could light pass?
   - Ⓐ a car window
   - Ⓑ a tree trunk
   - Ⓒ a brick wall
   - Ⓓ a piece of aluminum foil

6. Which of the following is a color in the rainbow?
   - Ⓔ pink
   - Ⓕ brown
   - Ⓖ red
   - Ⓗ black

Physical Science *(cont.)*

7. A compass works by using the force of
   - Ⓐ magnetism.
   - Ⓑ gravity.
   - Ⓒ the sun.
   - Ⓓ the tides.

11. If you stood in a cave and hollered "Happy New Year," you would most likely create
    - Ⓐ a sound.
    - Ⓑ an echo.
    - Ⓒ a disturbance.
    - Ⓓ a pitch.

8. The force that stops a bike when the brakes are applied is called
   - Ⓔ the stopping force.
   - Ⓕ inertia.
   - Ⓖ friction.
   - Ⓗ gravity.

12. Which part of our bodies receives the vibrations from the energy of sound?
    - Ⓔ eardrum
    - Ⓕ optic nerve
    - Ⓖ earlobe
    - Ⓗ brain wave

9. When a gas cools and turns into a liquid it is called
   - Ⓐ evaporation.
   - Ⓑ condensation.
   - Ⓒ precipitation.
   - Ⓓ water pressure.

13. The pitch of a tuba is probably
    - Ⓐ high.
    - Ⓑ average.
    - Ⓒ low.
    - Ⓓ fast.

10. When objects vibrate they create
    - Ⓔ friction.
    - Ⓕ gravity.
    - Ⓖ sound.
    - Ⓗ air currents.

14. Amplitude is the measure of
    - Ⓔ how large a wave is.
    - Ⓕ how frequent a wave is.
    - Ⓖ the pitch of a sound wave.
    - Ⓗ the depth of a wave.

STOP

Life Science

Directions: Fill in the answer circle for your choice.

Samples

A. Which types of animals have gills?

  Ⓐ mammals

  Ⓑ reptiles

  Ⓒ fish

  Ⓓ birds

B. An example of a cold-blooded animal is a

  Ⓐ snake.

  Ⓑ puppy.

  Ⓒ parrot.

  Ⓓ monkey.

---

1. Animals that have backbones are called

  Ⓐ invertebrates.

  Ⓑ vertebrates.

  Ⓒ strong.

  Ⓓ mammals.

2. Some characteristics of mammals are

  Ⓔ cold-blooded with no fur.

  Ⓕ warm-blooded with no fur.

  Ⓖ warm-blooded with fur or skin.

  Ⓗ cold-blooded with scales.

3. Hibernation is a kind of

  Ⓐ amphibian.

  Ⓑ deep sleep.

  Ⓒ scientist.

  Ⓓ exercise.

4. An animal that spends time on land and in water is called

  Ⓔ a good swimmer.

  Ⓕ a reptile.

  Ⓖ a frog.

  Ⓗ an amphibian.

5. Adaptations help animals

  Ⓐ grow.

  Ⓑ survive.

  Ⓒ play.

  Ⓓ breed.

6. On what animals would you expect to find blubber?

  Ⓔ the great apes

  Ⓕ marine mammals

  Ⓖ rain forest birds

  Ⓗ cold-blooded animals

7. Predatory animals usually have

  Ⓐ long tails.

  Ⓑ manes.

  Ⓒ sharp teeth and claws.

  Ⓓ spotted coats.

8. Which are the only animals on Earth to use verbal communication?

  Ⓔ humans

  Ⓕ all mammals

  Ⓖ gorillas

  Ⓗ none of these

9. A baby learning how to crawl is an example of
   Ⓐ learned behavior.
   Ⓑ locomotion.
   Ⓒ instinctive behavior.
   Ⓓ good muscle tone.

10. Animal offspring means
   Ⓔ the babies of animals.
   Ⓕ the parents of animals.
   Ⓖ the caretakers of animals in captivity.
   Ⓗ the adult stage of animals.

11. A caterpillar is one stage in the life cycle of what animal?
   Ⓐ tadpole
   Ⓑ spider
   Ⓒ butterfly
   Ⓓ adult caterpillar

12. An animal that eats dead animals is called a
   Ⓔ predator.
   Ⓕ scavenger.
   Ⓖ herbivore.
   Ⓗ hyena.

13. Birds flying south for the winter is an example of
   Ⓐ hibernation.
   Ⓑ incubation.
   Ⓒ gestation.
   Ⓓ migration.

14. The spots on a leopard are an example of
   Ⓔ beauty.
   Ⓕ camouflage.
   Ⓖ disease.
   Ⓗ endangered species.

15. What types of animals have mandibles?
   Ⓐ sharks
   Ⓑ mammals
   Ⓒ birds
   Ⓓ insects

16. What do fish use to help them swim?
   Ⓔ fins
   Ⓕ gills
   Ⓖ sonar
   Ⓗ plankton

17. Marsupials are mammals that possess
   Ⓐ gills.
   Ⓑ scales.
   Ⓒ pouches.
   Ⓓ opposable thumbs.

18. Echolocation is a type of
   Ⓔ nonverbal communication.
   Ⓕ verbal communication.
   Ⓖ hunting technique.
   Ⓗ dolphin.

19. Constriction is mostly used by what animals?
   Ⓐ birds
   Ⓑ crocodiles
   Ⓒ snakes
   Ⓓ mammals

20. When an animal becomes extinct it means
   Ⓔ it no longer exists on the planet.
   Ⓕ its existence is threatened.
   Ⓖ it is a dinosaur.
   Ⓗ it is plentiful.

Life Science *(cont.)*

Directions: Fill in the answer circles for your choices.

Samples

A Roots help plants get

- Ⓐ **water.**
- Ⓑ air.
- Ⓒ carbon dioxide.
- Ⓓ sunlight.

B Stem is to plant as

- Ⓔ wheels are to car.
- Ⓕ **veins are to people.**
- Ⓖ money is to bank.
- Ⓗ water is to ocean.

---

1. What substance do plants use to make seeds?
   - Ⓐ fertilizer
   - Ⓑ pollen
   - Ⓒ leaves
   - Ⓓ soil

2. Plants produce food by using
   - Ⓔ soil nutrients.
   - Ⓕ nutrients from water.
   - Ⓖ photosynthesis.
   - Ⓗ nutrients in the air.

3. Plants absorb
   - Ⓐ carbon dioxide.
   - Ⓑ oxygen.
   - Ⓒ carbon monoxide.
   - Ⓓ helium.

4. Plants release
   - Ⓔ carbon dioxide.
   - Ⓕ carbon monoxide.
   - Ⓖ hydrogen.
   - Ⓗ oxygen.

5. The stamen and the pistil are
   - Ⓐ roots and stems of the plant.
   - Ⓑ leaf systems.
   - Ⓒ the male and female parts of flowers.
   - Ⓓ taproots.

6. The basic needs of a plant or animal mean
   - Ⓔ the things it needs to survive.
   - Ⓕ the things it wants.
   - Ⓖ the things it likes.
   - Ⓗ sunlight only.

7. Another name for a seedling might be
   - Ⓐ organism.
   - Ⓑ sprout.
   - Ⓒ plant.
   - Ⓓ crop.

8. A bumble bee is an example of a
   - Ⓔ predator.
   - Ⓕ herbivore.
   - Ⓖ pollinator.
   - Ⓗ mammal.

9. Which of the following is used during photosynthesis?
   - Ⓐ soil
   - Ⓑ air
   - Ⓒ chlorophyll
   - Ⓓ pollen

10. Tree rings can be used to find out
    - Ⓔ how old a tree is.
    - Ⓕ how tall a tree is.
    - Ⓖ how beautiful a tree is.
    - Ⓗ how nutritious a tree is.

Life Science *(cont.)*

Directions: Fill in the answer circles for your choices.

Samples

A The driest ecosystems are

- Ⓐ rain forests.
- Ⓑ grasslands.
- **Ⓒ deserts.**
- Ⓓ woodlands

B Animals that are active at night are

- Ⓔ night owls.
- **Ⓕ nocturnal.**
- Ⓖ insomniac.
- Ⓗ bats.

---

1. Many desert animals are nocturnal because
   - Ⓐ they like to be out at night.
   - Ⓑ they feel safer at night.
   - Ⓒ it is cooler at night.
   - Ⓓ they can only see in the dark.

2. If you were walking through a desert, what kind of plants would you expect to find?
   - Ⓔ tall evergreen trees
   - Ⓕ flowering bushes
   - Ⓖ sparse brush close to the ground
   - Ⓗ grapevines

3. In an ecosystem, all living things are
   - Ⓐ cooperative.
   - Ⓑ interdependent.
   - Ⓒ friendly.
   - Ⓓ not cooperative.

4. The prairies of the United States are ecosystems called
   - Ⓔ the Great Plains.
   - Ⓕ the Interior Plains.
   - Ⓖ grasslands.
   - Ⓗ forests.

5. Deciduous, coniferous, and tropical are types of
   - Ⓐ forests.
   - Ⓑ savannahs.
   - Ⓒ deserts.
   - Ⓓ marshes.

6. Rain forests are typically located
   - Ⓔ near the equator.
   - Ⓕ near the North Pole.
   - Ⓖ near the South Pole.
   - Ⓗ at high altitudes.

7. A tree that loses its leaves is called
   - Ⓐ coniferous.
   - Ⓑ tropical.
   - Ⓒ sickly.
   - Ⓓ deciduous.

8. The trees most associated with Christmas are
   - Ⓔ coniferous.
   - Ⓕ oak trees.
   - Ⓖ tropical.
   - Ⓗ deciduous.

GO

Directions: Fill in the answer circles for your choices.

9. If you wanted to view the canopy of a rain forest you would have to
   Ⓐ look down.
   Ⓑ look to you right.
   Ⓒ look up.
   Ⓓ close your eyes.

10. Lakes, ponds, and swamps are examples of
    Ⓔ flowing water ecosystems.
    Ⓕ standing water ecosystems.
    Ⓖ marine ecosystems.
    Ⓗ oceans.

11. Coral reefs are usually found in
    Ⓐ warm tropical waters.
    Ⓑ cold tropical waters.
    Ⓒ ponds over ten feet in depth.
    Ⓓ ponds less that ten feet in depth.

12. A freshwater ecosystem means that the water does not contain a significant amount of
    Ⓔ oxygen.
    Ⓕ nitrogen.
    Ⓖ salt.
    Ⓗ fish.

13. You would expect to find a whale in
    Ⓐ a marine ecosystem.
    Ⓑ a freshwater ecosystem.
    Ⓒ a large lake.
    Ⓓ a swamp.

14. If one part of an ecosystem were destroyed, what might happen?
    Ⓔ Nothing at all.
    Ⓕ People would not come to visit.
    Ⓖ It would endanger the entire ecosystem.
    Ⓗ It would totally destroy the ecosystem.

STOP

Climate and Weather

Directions: Fill in the answer circles for your choices.

Samples

A Precipitation refers to
- Ⓐ rain
- Ⓑ snow
- Ⓒ sleet
- **Ⓓ All of these.**

B A meteorologist is a person who
- Ⓔ **studies the weather.**
- Ⓕ studies earthquakes.
- Ⓖ studies meteors.
- Ⓗ studies volcanoes.

1. The area on Earth that receives the most sunlight is
   - Ⓐ the North and South Poles.
   - Ⓑ the equator.
   - Ⓒ the oceans.
   - Ⓓ the mountains.

2. The area on Earth that receives the least amount of sunlight is around
   - Ⓔ the Prime Meridian.
   - Ⓕ the North and South Poles.
   - Ⓖ deserts.
   - Ⓗ beaches.

3. Climate refers to
   - Ⓐ the typical weather in a place over a long period of time.
   - Ⓑ day-to-day weather.
   - Ⓒ the atmosphere in a place.
   - Ⓓ snow fall.

4. The earth's atmosphere is comprised of
   - Ⓔ water.
   - Ⓕ air.
   - Ⓖ bellum.
   - Ⓗ clouds.

5. A barometer is used to measure
   - Ⓐ air speed.
   - Ⓑ air quality.
   - Ⓒ air pressure.
   - Ⓓ air pollution.

6. The largest source of energy for Earth is
   - Ⓔ water.
   - Ⓕ the sun.
   - Ⓖ stars.
   - Ⓗ fossil fuels.

7. Cirrus, cumulus, and stratus are types of
   - Ⓐ weather systems.
   - Ⓑ oceans.
   - Ⓒ fronts.
   - Ⓓ clouds.

8. Clouds are made-up of
   - Ⓔ water.
   - Ⓕ air.
   - Ⓖ debris.
   - Ⓗ cotton.

9. A cloud that exists close to the ground is called
   - Ⓐ fog.
   - Ⓑ haze.
   - Ⓒ condensation.
   - Ⓓ mist.

10. The jet stream is a strong
    - Ⓔ ocean current.
    - Ⓕ weather pattern.
    - Ⓖ wind current.
    - Ⓗ storm.

Geography

Directions: Fill in the answer circle for your choice.

Samples

A. A globe is shaped like a
- Ⓐ circle.
- Ⓑ cone.
- **Ⓒ sphere.**
- Ⓓ balloon

B. Cardinal directions are
- Ⓐ north and south.
- Ⓑ east and west.
- Ⓒ northeast and northwest.
- **Ⓓ Both A and B**

---

1. A person who makes maps is also called

   Ⓐ cartographer.

   Ⓑ an aviator.

   Ⓒ a surveyor.

   Ⓓ a seismologist.

2. A book in which you would expect to find a collection of maps is called

   Ⓔ a dictionary.

   Ⓕ an encyclopedia.

   Ⓖ an atlas.

   Ⓗ a web site.

3. Which imaginary line divides Earth into the Northern and Southern Hemispheres?

   Ⓐ Prime Meridian

   Ⓑ axis

   Ⓒ equator

   Ⓓ lines of longitude

4. Lines of latitude run from

   Ⓔ north to south.

   Ⓕ east to west.

   Ⓖ northeast to southeast.

   Ⓗ southwest to southeast.

5. The Prime Meridian divides Earth into

   Ⓐ the Eastern and Western Hemispheres.

   Ⓑ the Northern and Southern Hemispheres.

   Ⓒ regions.

   Ⓓ continents.

6. If you traveled to the southernmost point on Earth you would be

   Ⓔ in Antarctica.

   Ⓕ at the North Pole.

   Ⓖ at the South Pole.

   Ⓗ in Australia

Directions: Fill in the answer circle for your choice.

7. If you were in the country of Egypt and wanted to travel to Morocco, in which direction would you have to travel?

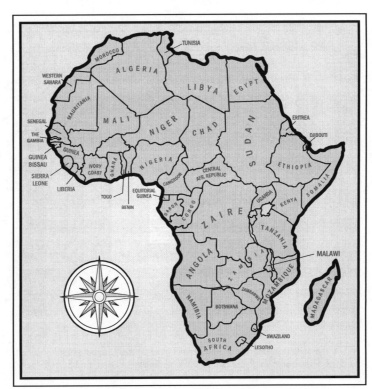

Ⓐ east

Ⓑ north

Ⓒ south

Ⓓ west

8. On what continent is China located?

Ⓔ Asia

Ⓕ Europe

Ⓖ North America

Ⓗ Africa

9. In what two hemispheres is the United States located?

Ⓐ northern and western

Ⓑ northern and eastern

Ⓒ southern and eastern

Ⓓ southern and western

ⒼⓄ

Directions: Fill in the answer circle for your choice.

10. If you were in the state of Kansas and you wanted to travel to Oregon, in which direction would you have to travel?

Ⓔ northwest

Ⓕ due north

Ⓖ west

Ⓗ southwest

---

11. If you say that your school is next to the shopping center, then you are speaking about its

Ⓐ absolute location.

Ⓑ relative location.

Ⓒ address.

Ⓓ proximity.

---

12. 721 Chestnut Street is an example of

Ⓔ a relative location.

Ⓕ map coordinates.

Ⓖ an absolute location.

Ⓗ directions.

Directions: Fill in the answer circle for your choice.

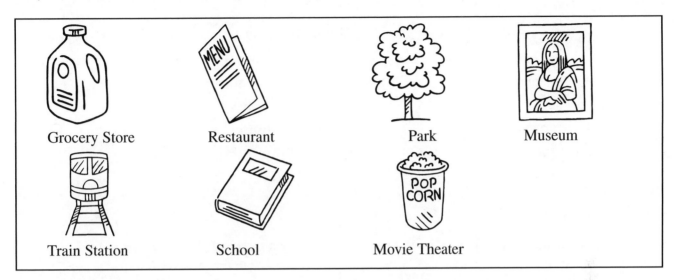

Grocery Store   Restaurant   Park   Museum

Train Station   School   Movie Theater

13. According to this legend, for what does this symbol stand?

Ⓐ school

Ⓑ grocery store

Ⓒ park

Ⓓ museum

14. According to this legend, for what does this symbol stand?

Ⓔ bus stop

Ⓕ restaurant

Ⓖ movie theater

Ⓗ train station

15. Saying that the bookshelf is to your left is an example of

Ⓐ personal directions.

Ⓑ relative directions.

Ⓒ cardinal directions.

Ⓓ intermediate directions.

Geography *(cont.)*

Directions: Fill in the answer circles for your choices.

Samples

A. Prairies in the United States are located

Ⓐ in New England.

Ⓑ in Florida.

Ⓒ in the Midwest.

Ⓓ in California.

B. The number of people in a region is called

Ⓔ population.

Ⓕ density.

Ⓖ census.

Ⓗ resources.

---

1. Which state is not found in the Midwest region of the United States?

Ⓐ Nebraska

Ⓑ Kansas

Ⓒ Oregon

Ⓓ Ohio

2. With which natural resource is Texas most associated?

Ⓔ lumber

Ⓕ coal

Ⓖ oil

Ⓗ fishing

3. In which United States region is Alaska?

Ⓐ northeast

Ⓑ west

Ⓒ southwest

Ⓓ Alaska is not part of any region.

4. Why are so many major cities in the United States located near rivers?

Ⓔ People like to live near water.

Ⓕ Rivers are used for transporting goods and people.

Ⓖ Rivers are nice to look at.

Ⓗ Rivers are easier to build along.

5. Which region of the United States is often referred to as "the breadbasket"?

Ⓐ Southeast

Ⓑ Northwest

Ⓒ Midwest

Ⓓ Southwest

6. Puerto Rico is

Ⓔ a territory of the United States.

Ⓕ a commonwealth of the United States.

Ⓖ the 52nd state.

Ⓗ an independent nation.

GO

Directions: Fill in the answer circles for your choices.

7. If you wanted to visit the Appalachian Mountains, to which region would you have to travel?

   Ⓐ Pennsylvania

   Ⓑ Northeast

   Ⓒ South

   Ⓓ California Region

8. The combined areas of Boston; New York; Philadelphia; Baltimore; and Washington, DC are called

   Ⓔ an urban region.

   Ⓕ densely populated.

   Ⓖ a megalopolis.

   Ⓗ a bunch of big cities.

9. What type of industry is likely to exist around the Great Lakes?

   Ⓐ oil drilling

   Ⓑ coal mining

   Ⓒ farming

   Ⓓ fishing

10. Orange juice, refined oil, and automobiles are examples of

    Ⓔ products.

    Ⓕ natural resources.

    Ⓖ human resources.

    Ⓗ nonrenewable.

11. Which river flows into the Gulf of Mexico?

    Ⓐ Delaware

    Ⓑ Snake

    Ⓒ Mississippi

    Ⓓ Colorado

12. What is located in the Southwest region that would attract so many tourists?

    Ⓔ The Grand Canyon

    Ⓕ Disney World

    Ⓖ Statue of Liberty

    Ⓗ Niagara Falls

13. What group of people typically lives on reservations?

    Ⓐ immigrants

    Ⓑ Native Americans

    Ⓒ Inuit

    Ⓓ Sioux only

14. Which region of the United States experiences the most earthquakes?

    Ⓔ Northeast

    Ⓕ West

    Ⓖ Midwest

    Ⓗ Southwest

United States Government

Directions: Fill in the answer circles for your choices.

Samples

A. The Untied States is a

Ⓐ **republic**

Ⓑ monarchy.

Ⓒ dictatorship.

Ⓓ oligarchy.

B. The branches of government are

Ⓐ executive.

Ⓑ judicial.

Ⓒ legislative.

Ⓓ **All of these.**

---

1. In a republic,

   Ⓐ a president is appointed by the Senate.

   Ⓑ citizens vote for public officials.

   Ⓒ a council rules the country.

   Ⓓ a king and queen preside over the country.

2. The Congress is also called

   Ⓔ the legislative branch.

   Ⓕ the executive branch.

   Ⓖ the judicial branch.

   Ⓗ the central branch.

3. The Congress is comprised of

   Ⓐ the Senate.

   Ⓑ the House of Representatives.

   Ⓒ both the House of Representatives and the Senate.

   Ⓓ the president and vice president.

4. Each state has how many senators?

   Ⓔ two

   Ⓕ four

   Ⓖ It depends on the population of the state

   Ⓗ six

5. The main job of Congress is

   Ⓐ to enforce the laws.

   Ⓑ to create the laws.

   Ⓒ to veto the laws.

   Ⓓ to get votes.

6. The President is part of what branch of government?

   Ⓔ legislative

   Ⓕ judicial

   Ⓖ executive

   Ⓗ Congress

7. If the President vetoes a law, it means that he or she has

   Ⓐ signed it into law.

   Ⓑ rejected it.

   Ⓒ asked for more details about the law.

   Ⓓ written the law himself or herself.

8. How do Supreme Court Justices get their jobs?

   Ⓔ They are elected by the people.

   Ⓕ They are elected by the Congress.

   Ⓖ They are selected by the President and approved by the Senate.

   Ⓗ They elect each other.

STOP

Student Answer Sheet

Name _____   Name _____

Page Number _____   Page Number _____

1.	Ⓐ	Ⓑ	Ⓒ	Ⓓ		1.	Ⓐ	Ⓑ	Ⓒ	Ⓓ	Ⓔ
2.	Ⓔ	Ⓕ	Ⓖ	Ⓗ		2.	Ⓕ	Ⓖ	Ⓗ	Ⓘ	Ⓙ
3.	Ⓐ	Ⓑ	Ⓒ	Ⓓ		3.	Ⓐ	Ⓑ	Ⓒ	Ⓓ	Ⓔ
4.	Ⓔ	Ⓕ	Ⓖ	Ⓗ		4.	Ⓕ	Ⓖ	Ⓗ	Ⓘ	Ⓙ
5.	Ⓐ	Ⓑ	Ⓒ	Ⓓ		5.	Ⓐ	Ⓑ	Ⓒ	Ⓓ	Ⓔ
6.	Ⓔ	Ⓕ	Ⓖ	Ⓗ		6.	Ⓕ	Ⓖ	Ⓗ	Ⓘ	Ⓙ
7.	Ⓐ	Ⓑ	Ⓒ	Ⓓ		7.	Ⓐ	Ⓑ	Ⓒ	Ⓓ	Ⓔ
8.	Ⓔ	Ⓕ	Ⓖ	Ⓗ		8.	Ⓕ	Ⓖ	Ⓗ	Ⓘ	Ⓙ
9.	Ⓐ	Ⓑ	Ⓒ	Ⓓ		9.	Ⓐ	Ⓑ	Ⓒ	Ⓓ	Ⓔ
10.	Ⓔ	Ⓕ	Ⓖ	Ⓗ		10.	Ⓕ	Ⓖ	Ⓗ	Ⓘ	Ⓙ
11.	Ⓐ	Ⓑ	Ⓒ	Ⓓ		11.	Ⓐ	Ⓑ	Ⓒ	Ⓓ	Ⓔ
12.	Ⓔ	Ⓕ	Ⓖ	Ⓗ		12.	Ⓕ	Ⓖ	Ⓗ	Ⓘ	Ⓙ
13.	Ⓐ	Ⓑ	Ⓒ	Ⓓ		13.	Ⓐ	Ⓑ	Ⓒ	Ⓓ	Ⓔ
14.	Ⓔ	Ⓕ	Ⓖ	Ⓗ		14.	Ⓕ	Ⓖ	Ⓗ	Ⓘ	Ⓙ
15.	Ⓐ	Ⓑ	Ⓒ	Ⓓ		15.	Ⓐ	Ⓑ	Ⓒ	Ⓓ	Ⓔ
16.	Ⓔ	Ⓕ	Ⓖ	Ⓗ		16.	Ⓕ	Ⓖ	Ⓗ	Ⓘ	Ⓙ
17.	Ⓐ	Ⓑ	Ⓒ	Ⓓ		17.	Ⓐ	Ⓑ	Ⓒ	Ⓓ	Ⓔ
18.	Ⓔ	Ⓕ	Ⓖ	Ⓗ		18.	Ⓕ	Ⓖ	Ⓗ	Ⓘ	Ⓙ
19.	Ⓐ	Ⓑ	Ⓒ	Ⓓ		19.	Ⓐ	Ⓑ	Ⓒ	Ⓓ	Ⓔ
20.	Ⓔ	Ⓕ	Ⓖ	Ⓗ		20.	Ⓕ	Ⓖ	Ⓗ	Ⓘ	Ⓙ
21.	Ⓐ	Ⓑ	Ⓒ	Ⓓ		21.	Ⓐ	Ⓑ	Ⓒ	Ⓓ	Ⓔ
22.	Ⓔ	Ⓕ	Ⓖ	Ⓗ		22.	Ⓕ	Ⓖ	Ⓗ	Ⓘ	Ⓙ
23.	Ⓐ	Ⓑ	Ⓒ	Ⓓ		23.	Ⓐ	Ⓑ	Ⓒ	Ⓓ	Ⓔ
24.	Ⓔ	Ⓕ	Ⓖ	Ⓗ		24.	Ⓕ	Ⓖ	Ⓗ	Ⓘ	Ⓙ
25.	Ⓐ	Ⓑ	Ⓒ	Ⓓ		25.	Ⓐ	Ⓑ	Ⓒ	Ⓓ	Ⓔ

Answer Key

Pages 14–15
1. B
2. G
3. E
4. G
5. D
6. F
7. B
8. G

Pages 20–21
1. B literal
2. G literal
3. D inferential
4. E literal
5. C analytical

Pages 23–24
1. B
2. G
3. D
4. E
5. B
6. F
7. D
8. F

Pages 25–26
1. D
2. H
3. A
4. E
5. B
6. G
7. B
8. G

Page 27
1. C
2. E
3. C
4. E
5. A
6. E

7. A
8. E
9. C
10. D
11. B
12. F

Page 28
1. A
2. E
3. A
4. F
5. B
6. D
7. A
8. F
9. A
10. E
11. C
12. D

Page 29
1. B
2. F
3. B
4. F
5. A
6. E
7. A
8. F
9. C
10. F
11. A
12. E

Page 30
1. B
2. F
3. A
4. E
5. C
6. D
7. C
8. E
9. A
10. F
11. B
12. E

Page 31
1. C
2. E
3. C
4. G
5. D
6. E

Page 32
1. C
2. F
3. A
4. F
5. A
6. F

Page 33
1. B
2. G
3. C
4. G
5. D
6. E

Page 34

1. A
2. G
3. D
4. F
5. A
6. H

Page 35

1. B
2. F
3. C
4. H
5. D
6. G
7. B
8. E

Page 36

1. B
2. G
3. A
4. F
5. B
6. G
7. B
8. H

Page 37

1. A
2. F
3. C
4. H
5. B
6. G
7. B
8. E
9. D
10. F

Page 38

1. B
2. H
3. A
4. G
5. B
6. E
7. D
8. F
9. A
10. F

Page 39

1. C
2. E
3. C
4. E
5. C
6. E
7. C
8. H

Page 40

1. A
2. H
3. C
4. H
5. B
6. H
7. A
8. G

Page 41

1. A
2. H
3. B
4. G
5. B
6. E
7. A
8. F

Page 42

1. B
2. F
3. A
4. H
5. B
6. E
7. D
8. F

Page 44

1. C
2. G
3. A
4. F
5. B
6. E
7. B
8. G

Page 46

1. C
2. F
3. C
4. G
5. A
6. F
7. A
8. H
9. C
10. F

Page 48

1. A
2. F
3. C
4. F
5. C
6. H
7. A
8. H
9. B
10. G

Page 50

1. B
2. G
3. A
4. H
5. A
6. F
7. B
8. G
9. D
10. G

Pages 51–52

1. C
2. E
3. E
4. G
5. C
6. H

Pages 53–54

1. A
2. F
3. A
4. H
5. B
6. E
7. C
8. G
9. A
10. G

Page 55

1. D
2. G
3. B
4. H
5. A
6. H

Page 56

1. B
2. G
3. C
4. E
5. B
6. E

Page 58

1. A
2. F
3. D
4. G
5. A
6. F

Page 60

1. C
2. F
3. B
4. G
5. A
6. G
7. C
8. E

Page 61

1. B
2. H
3. A
4. H
5. A
6. G

Pages 62–63

1. B
2. H
3. A
4. F
5. C
6. E
7. C
8. F

Page 64

1. C
2. E
3. B
4. G
5. A
6. H

Page 65

1. C
2. F
3. B
4. F
5. A
6. H

Page 66

1. A
2. F
3. B
4. F
5. D
6. E
7. C
8. E
9. B
10. E

Page 67

1. A
2. F
3. A
4. H
5. B
6. E
7. A
8. H
9. A
10. E

Page 68

1. A
2. H
3. B
4. G
5. D
6. E
7. C
8. G

Page 69

1. A
2. H
3. E
4. F
5. B
6. H
7. B
8. J

Pages 70–71

1. C
2. F
3. C
4. F
5. D
6. G
7. A
8. F
9. D
10. H

Pages 73–74

1. B
2. F
3. D
4. E
5. D
6. F
7. A
8. D
9. F
10. I
11. C
12. J
13. F

Pages 76–77

1. E
2. J
3. D
4. H
5. D
6. J
7. D
8. H
9. A
10. H
11. A
12. I
13. A

Pages 78–79

1. B
2. H
3. A
4. I
5. D
6. H
7. E
8. F
9. C
10. G
11. E
12. J
13. B
14. H
15. D
16. J
17. D
18. H
19. D
20. G

Page 80

1. C
2. H
3. A
4. F
5. E
6. G
7. A
8. F
9. B
10. H

Pages 81–82

1. B
2. G
3. A
4. G
5. D
6. F
7. D
8. H

Page 83

1. C
2. G
3. D
4. H
5. B
6. H
7. C
8. I

Pages 84–85

1. A
2. H
3. B
4. H
5. A
6. H
7. E
8. I
9. B
10. F

11. C
12. F

Pages 86–87

1. A
2. H
3. C
4. I
5. A
6. G
7. C
8. F

Page 88

1. D
2. E
3. D
4. E
5. B
6. E
7. A
8. E

Pages 89–90

1. B
2. H
3. A
4. G
5. B
6. G
7. A
8. E
9. A
10. H
11. C
12. G

Page 91

1. B
2. G
3. B
4. H
5. A
6. E

7. A
8. G
9. C
10. E

Page 92

1. C
2. E
3. C
4. H
5. A
6. F
7. D
8. G

Pages 93–94

1. C
2. E
3. C
4. H
5. A
6. H
7. B
8. G
9. C
10. G

Page 95

1. C
2. H
3. D
4. G
5. A
6. E
7. B
8. G

Answer Key (cont.)

Pages 96–97
1. B
2. F
3. C
4. E
5. C
6. E
7. C
8. G
9. D
10. H
11. C
12. E
13. D
14. E

Page 98
1. C
2. E
3. A
4. G
5. D
6. E

Pages 99–100
1. C
2. E
3. D
4. H
5. A
6. H
7. B
8. H

Page 101
1. A
2. F
3. A
4. G
5. C
6. E
7. B
8. G

Pages 102–106
1. B
2. E
3. A
4. H
5. B
6. G
7. D
8. E
9. A
10. G
11. C
12. F
13. D
14. G
15. A
16. F
17. A

Pages 107–108
1. C
2. H
3. B
4. E
5. C
6. G
7. D
8. F

Pages 109–111
1. D
2. F
3. C
4. E
5. D
6. E
7. C
8. H
9. A
10. E
11. G
12. E
13. B
14. E
15. D
16. E

Page 112
1. C
2. F
3. A
4. J
5. A
6. G
7. B
8. F

Answer Key (cont.)

Pages 113–114

1. D
2. E
3. C
4. H
5. D
6. E
7. B
8. F
9. A
10. E
11. B
12. H
13. C
14. E
15. C
16. E
17. C
18. H
19. C
20. E

Pages 115–116

1. C
2. E
3. B
4. G
5. D
6. E
7. C
8. H
9. C
10. E
11. B
12. G
13. D
14. G
15. D
16. E
17. B
18. E
19. B
20. G

Pages 117–118

1. B
2. H
3. B
4. E
5. B
6. E
7. D
8. E
9. C
10. E
11. C
12. F
13. A
14. G
15. D
16. G
17. A
18. H
19. B
20. F

Page 119

1. C
2. F
3. A
4. F
5. A
6. G
7. D
8. E
9. A
10. H

Pages 120–121

1. C
2. H
3. A
4. F
5. A
6. G
7. A
8. G
9. B
10. G
11. B
12. E
13. C
14. E

Pages 122–123

1. B
2. G
3. B
4. H
5. B
6. F
7. C
8. E
9. C
10. E
11. C
12. F
13. D
14. F
15. D
16. E
17. C
18. E
19. C
20. E

Page 124

1. B
2. G
3. A
4. H
5. C
6. E
7. B
8. G
9. C
10. E

Pages 125–126

1. C
2. G
3. B
4. G
5. A
6. E
7. D
8. E
9. C
10. F
11. A
12. G
13. A
14. G

Page 127

1. B
2. F
3. A
4. F
5. C
6. F
7. D
8. E
9. A
10. G

Answer Key (cont.)

Pages 128–131

1. A
2. G
3. C
4. F
5. A
6. G
7. D
8. E
9. A
10. E
11. B
12. G
13. C
14. H
15. B

Pages 132–133

1. C
2. G
3. B
4. F
5. C
6. F
7. B
8. G
9. D
10. E
11. C
12. E
13. B
14. F

Page 134

1. B
2. E
3. C
4. E
5. B
6. G
7. B
8. G